SOUL WHISPERER

By Almas Taufiq

Your ultimate guide to spirituality in the digital age
To manifest the secrets of your soul

Book 1
Stories 1 to 5 Derived from the Unique and Unparalleled

Mathnavi i Manavi
By
Maulana Jalaluddin Muhammad Rumi R.A.

With commentary based on the Incomparable
Kaleed i Mathnavi
by Shaykh Hazrat Ashraf Ali Thanvi R.A.

SOUL WHISPERER

Written by: Almas Taufiq
                 Email: almastaufiq@gmail.com
                 Facebook: /almastaufiq
                 Website: www.almastaufiq.com
                 LinkedIn: /almastaufiq

Distributer: Al-Aaizah
                 www.alaaizah.org

Edition: 2020

ISBN #   978-969-9935-11-4

Table of Contents

Foreword

All praise is due to Allahﷻ, who created such pious ulamaa and saints in the ummah of the Prophetﷺ, who guided the people with wisdom. Maulana Rumi, may Allah have mercy on him, is one of those great scholars who recognized the nation's spiritual ailments and advocated for such an effective reformation that it is difficult to find an example.

This is a translation of a Persian Mystical poetry book "Ma'aarif e Mathnavi", written by Maulana Rumi, that the author "Madam Almas Taufiq" has written in an excellent style with a very good layout. It displays a remarkable manner for the English readers, such that on the one hand is the best source of motivation, and on the other is a powerful medicine for the present era's psychological confusions and spiritual deficiency in the new generation.

She chose the best thing to work on and then did the work in the best way. Ma Sha Allah

The selection of words, the combination of phrases, and the structure of the sentences are outstanding that end up with a tremendous positive, motivational effect.

You can't pass without admiring the detailed and meaningful interpretations of the worth considering passages that have made this book a top priority in English work on the subject.

This is a worth recommending and worth reading work that suits the current study mood of the present time. This book must be placed on the nearest shelf in the library of every knowledgeable person.

May Allahﷻ grant acceptance and popularity to the book, and make this book a source of guidance for humanity, as well as a source of success in both worlds for Madam Almas Taufiq as well as for us. May He grant us all the levels of spirituality that can help us gain His pleasure. Aameen.

Maulana Mufti Mohammad Osama Sarfraz
Usama.sarfaraz@maju.edu.pk

Maulana Mufti Usama Sarfaraz is a graduate of Mahd-ul-Khalil and has 16 years of teaching experience in renowned madrasahs. He is also managing Madrasah Nur-ul-Quran (with branches in Saddar, Gulshan, Malir & Shah Faisal Colony) since 20 years. In addition, he is a khateeb and senior imam at Jamia Masjid La'aiba, Karachi. He is also a lecturer at Mohammad Ali Jinnah University and founder of Noor Model School.

With the name of Allah, the Most Beneficent, the Most Merciful

وما توفيقي إلا بالله

(Al-Quran 11:88)

Ruminations on Rumi R.A.

You are not a drop in the ocean;
You are the entire ocean in a drop. Rumi

These lines by the prestigious Persian poet Jami portray the Mathnavi as such:

What can I say to describe that excellent - one,
Who's not a prophet, but came with a sacred text.
The Spiritual Mathnawi of Mevlevi (my Lord) -
Tis' the Quran in the language of Pahlavi.

Rumi's *Mathnavi* is widely recognized as the greatest Sufi poem ever written. The thirteenth-century Muslim mystic Rumi composed his work for the benefit of his disciples in the Sufi order named after him, better known as the whirling dervishes. In order to convey his message of divine love and unity he threaded together entertaining stories and penetrating homilies. Drawing from folk tales as well as sacred history, Rumi's poem is often funny as well as spiritually profound.

"The Masnavi, Masnavi-I Ma'navi or Mesnevi (Turkish), also written Mathnawi Ma'navi, or Mathnavi, is an extensive poem written in Persian by Jalal al-Din Muhammad Rumi, the celebrated Persian Sufi saint and poet. It is one of the best known and most influential works of both Sufism and Persian literature. The Masnavi is a series of six books of poetry that amount to about 25,000 verses or 50,000 lines. It is a spiritual writing that teaches how to reach the goal of being in true love with God.

The title Masnavi-I Ma'navi means "Rhyming Couplets of Profound Spiritual Meaning."

Rumi himself referred to the Masnavi as "the roots of the roots of the roots of the (Islamic) Religion."

The Masnavi is a poetic collection of rambling anecdotes and stories derived from the Quran, hadith sources, and everyday tales. Stories are told to illustrate a point and each moral is discussed in detail. It incorporates a variety of Islamic wisdom but primarily focuses on emphasizing inward personal Sufi interpretation. This work by Rumi is referred to as a "sober" Sufi text. It reasonably presents the various dimensions of Sufi spiritual life and advises disciples on their spiritual paths.

More generally, it is aimed at anyone who has time to sit down and ponder the meaning of life and existence.

The Masnavi was a Sufi masterpiece started during the final years of Rumi's life. He began dictating the first book around the age of 54 around the year 1258 AD and continued composing verses until his death in 1273. The sixth and final book would remain incomplete.

Each book consists of about 4,000 verses and contains its own prose, introduction and prologue. Considering there are no epilogues, one must read the proceeding volumes to fully benefit from the wisdom presented by Rumi. Some scholars suggest that in addition to the incomplete work of Book 6, there might be a seventh volume.

The six books of the Masnavi can be divided into three groups of two because each pair is linked by a common theme:

Books 1 and 2: They are principally concerned with the self, the lower carnal self, and its self-deception and evil tendencies.

Books 3 and 4: These books share the principal themes of Reason and Knowledge. These two themes are personified by Rumi in the Biblical and Quranic figure of the Prophet Moses.

Books 5 and 6: These last two books are joined by the universal ideal that man must deny his physical earthly existence to understand God's existence.

Mawlana Jalal-ad-Din Muhammad Rumi, also known as Mawlana Jalal-ad-Din Muhammad Balhi, but known to the English - speaking world simply as Rumi, (September 30, 1207 - December 17, 1273), was a 13th century Persian (Tadjik) poet, Islamic jurist and theologian. Rumi is a descriptive name meaning "the Roman" since he lived most parts of his life in Anatolia which had been part of the Roman Empire until the Seljuq conquest two centuries earlier.

Modern scholars now believe that Rumi was probably born in 1207 CE in Wakhsh/Vakhsh (in modern day Tajikistan, then under rule of Ghurids), while traditional sources claim his father's family had for several generations lived in Balkh (in modern day Afghanistan, then incorporated into the Khwarezm Empire around 1205 CE). Both these cities were at the time included in the Greater Persian cultural sphere of Khorasan, the easternmost province of historical Persia.

His birthplace and first language both indicate a Persian heritage. Due to quarrels between different dynasties in Khorasan, opposition to Khwarizmid Shahs who were considered devious by Rumi's father or fear of the impending Mongol cataclysm, Baha-e Walad (Rumi's father) decided to migrate westwards. Rumi traveled west with his father and family, first performing the Hajj and eventually settling in Konya (In modern day Turkey, then in the Seljuk Sultanate of Rum), where he lived most of his life, composed one of the crowning glories of Persian literature and profoundly affected the culture of the area. New Persian (also called Dari-Persian or Dari), a widely understood vernacular of Middle Persian, has its linguistic origin in the Fars Province of modern Iran. A Dari-Persian literary renaissance (in the 8th/9th century) started in regions of Sistan, Khorasan and Transoxiana and by the 10th/11th century, it overtook Arabic as the literary and cultural language in the Persian Islamic world.

He lived most of his life under the Seljuk Sultanate of Rum, where he produced his works and died in 1273 CE in Konya. He was buried in Konya and his shrine became a place of pilgrimage. The shrine is now known as the Mevlana Museum. Following his death, his followers and his son Sultan Walad founded the

Mevlevi Order, also known as the Whirling Dervishes, who are known for their famous ceremony called the sema.[i]

"The Mevlevi order issues an invitation to people of all backgrounds:

<blockquote>
Come, come, whoever you are,

Wanderer, idolater, worshipper of fire.

Come even though you have

Broken your vows a thousand times.

Come, and come yet again.

Ours is not a caravan of despair.
</blockquote>

Many of Rumi's poems suggest the importance of outward religious observance and the primacy of the Qur'an.[ii]

<blockquote>
Flee to God's Qur'an, take refuge in it.

There with the spirits of the prophets merge.

The Book conveys the prophets' circumstances,

Those fish of the pure sea of Majesty.[iii]
</blockquote>

Rumi states:

<blockquote>
I am the servant of the Qur'an as long as I have life.

I am the dust on the path of Muhammadﷺ, the Chosen one.

If anyone quotes anything except this from my sayings,

I am quit of him and outraged by these words.[iv]
</blockquote>

Rumi also states:

I "sewed" my two eyes shut from [desires for] this world and the next – this I learned from Muhammadﷺ.

Why did I choose the Mathnavi for my book?

My life's journey has been long and arduous, yet filled with exhilaration and triumph, with the grace of my Lord. It has been a journey of learning and growth. Every step has shown me a new way to live, a better way to live, and has gradually taken me from darkness to light. I have lived a blessed life, and yet, there was nothing in my early years to give an insight to anything in the future other than complete doom. As I found new meaning and purpose to my life, I knew for sure that I had to share the source of my enlightenment and my learning with the world, for whatever it was worth. Maybe somebody floundering in the storms of life, or even somebody trying to find a new purpose to life will find some source of guidance or inspiration from my writing.

This thought kept taking shape. I was searching for where to begin writing, and then I just woke up one morning with the word Mathnavi going around in my head! I've been an avid follower of Rumi quotes but had never read the Mathnavi itself. First, I was perplexed as I couldn't make a connection and didn't know why this word was circulating in my mind. As the day progressed it gained strength. Of course, I Googled (!) and found quite a few translations and commentaries of the book online. I started reading and as I read, I knew I had to share this inspiring and phenomenal spiritual composition with others, who, like me, had been deprived of such spiritual awakening through it. I called up my mentor and teacher, Honourable Mufti Maulana Shafiq Arif and shared with him. He was full of joy and eagerness. He encouraged me to definitely work on the Mathnavi as it was a much needed message of love and spirituality for the millennials. He suggested I translate the commentary from Kaleed i Mathnavi by Shaykh Hazrat Ashraf Ali Thanvi, which is the most comprehensive and detailed ever written. It is written in the early twentieth century Urdu, which is too heavy and archaic for most young Urdu readers and virtually impossible to fathom for non-Urdu readers.

He said, "Mathnavi is the book after the book of Allah﷾."

How did I do it?

I am weak and the Mathnavi is gigantic, and the Kaleed is equally colossal. It felt like I was trying to swim in an ocean of knowledge, spirituality and wonder. I had nothing on my side except Divine guidance, a meagre understanding of Arabic, Persian, the Quran and Sunnah, and the blessings of my mentor. To say it in Rumi's own words, when a small hare defeated a cruel lion and all the animals of the jungle asked him how he did it, this is what he said:

"O Sirs," said he, "It was God's aid;
Else, who in the world is a hare?
He bestowed power on me and gave light to my heart:
The light in my heart gave strength to hand and foot."

From God come enhancements,
From God also come changes.
God in course and turn
Is ever displaying this aid to doubters and seers.
Take heed! Do not exult in a kingdom bestowed in turns.
O you who are the bondsman of instability,
Do not act as though you were free!

In this amazing journey of self-discovery and the glorious path to a life well lived, my biggest source of inspiration along with my faith, teachers, family and friends, were Maulana Rumi and Shaykh Thanvi. I had never read the Mathnavi, but had followed Rumi's quotes all my life and used them as my guiding light to a sincere life of purpose. Shaykh Thanvi's books were the most valuable source of true guidance for my deepest learning of Quran, Sunnah (Prophetic narrations) and a spiritual way of life. I am truly humbled beyond measure to be given the chance to share the combined wisdom of both these icons of the highest spiritual standards and the sincerest seekers of the True Path.

The Mathnavi, a collection of poems on spirituality, truly lighted up my way. I aspire to share excerpts from this work that I found most inspiring, and hope that, like me, you will find illumination to ignite the sparks, that will help you soar to new heights of magnificence and a life of true worth.

"Rumi's Mathnavi is in many ways a roadmap of spiritual growth. It begins with the condition of so many of us: being broken, homesick, cut off, alone, down and out, and unsure of our own worth. The narrative moves through the purification of the heart, the cleansing experience of love, before moving to the state of being a real human being. The story that the Mathnavi tells is the path that all of us have to go through, moving from brokenness to healing, from spiritually feeling worthless and cut off to being wholehearted. That is the whole goal of the spiritual path: not divinity, but full humanity.[v]

In Rumi's own words:

> On the seeker's path, wise men and fools are one.
> In His love, brothers and strangers are one.
> Go on! Drink the wine of the Beloved!
> In that faith, Muslims and pagans are one.[vi]

"According to the Quran, Prophet Muhammadﷺ is a mercy sent by God to the Aalameen (to all creation), including humanity overall (Al-Quran 21:107). In regards to this, Rumi states:

The Light of Muhammadﷺ does not abandon a Zoroastrian or Jew in the world. May the shade of his good fortune shine upon everyone! He brings all of those who are led astray into the Way out of the desert.[vii]

I am the servant of the Qur'an as long as I have life. I am the dust on the path of Muhammadﷺ, the Chosen one. If anyone quotes anything except this from my sayings, I am quit of him and outraged by these words.[viii]

His Mathnavi contains anecdotes and stories derived largely from the Quran and the hadith (Prophetic narrations), as well as everyday tales.[ix]

Kaleedi Mathnavi

Kaleedi Mathnavi is a complete commentary on the Mathnavi by Shaykh Thanvi in the Urdu language. It is in 24 volumes and each volume has 300 to 500 pages. It is the most in-depth explanation of the Mathnavi ever to have been written by one of the greatest scholars of the last two centuries. It is like the synthesis of two giants of the world of Islam and Spirituality.

"Muhammad Ashraf 'Ali Thanvi (August 19, 1863 – July 4, 1943) was an Indian Sunni Islamic scholar. He was a descendant of Umar bin Khattab from his father's side and a descendant of Ali bin Abdul Muttalib from his mother's side. He lost his mother at the age of 5 and was raised by his father with special care and attention. His father taught him and his younger brother (Akbar 'Ali) discipline and good character. He loved offering Salah and congregation and abstained from playing with other children. He started tahajjud (late night prayer) from the age of 12 or 13. He also loved Dhikr (meditation and remembrance of Allah﷾). Shaykh Thanvi received his early education in the Persian language, memorization of the Qur'aan and elementary Arabic. He then got admitted in Darul Uloom Deoband India in 1295 and studied there for 5 years, graduating in 1301 AH (1884). During his student life, he received special attention from the great scholars and teachers like Mawlana Ya'qoob Nanotvi, Grand Mufti 'Azeezu-R-Rahmaan 'Uthmani, and Mahmud al-Hasan. He was tried and tested by Rashid Ahmad

Gangohi at his graduation. During his stay at Deoband, he refused invitations from his relatives and abstained from mixing with other students. He was one of the best reciters of the Qur'aan and was taught by Qāriʾ 'Abdullaah Muhaajir Makki, who was famous amongst the reciters of Arabia.

After his graduation, Hazrat Thanvi taught high level books of religious sciences. Over a short period of time, he acquired a reputable position as a religious scholar of Sufism among other subject. His teaching attracted numerous students and his research and publications became well known in Islamic institutions. During these years, he traveled to various cities and villages, delivering lectures in the hope of reforming people. Printed versions of his lectures and discourses usually became available shortly after these tours. Until then, few Islamic scholars had had their lectures printed and widely circulated in their own lifetimes. The desire to reform the masses intensified in him as he grew older.

Eventually, Hazrat Thanvi retired from teaching and devoted himself to reestablishing the spiritual centre of his shaikh in Thāna Bhāwan.[x]

How to use this book?

I've selected excerpts that helped me search for new meaning in my connection with Allahﷻ and myself, and also, as I thought of relevance to today's lifestyle and thinking. You can read it page by page or just open to any page and find inspiration for the day.

I pray to the Almighty for acceptance of this humble effort and forgiveness for any transgressions. May this book be a source of guidance for the mind, body and soul to a life of spiritual existence and true worth, which is the sincere aspiration of the human soul.

......هذا من فضل ربي..

This is from the grace of my Lord.

(27:40 ....Relevant portion of verse quoted)

Mathnavi Manavi Book 1

In The Name Of Allah﷾ The Merciful The Compassionate

This is the Book of the Mathnavi, which is the roots of the roots of the roots of the Way in respect of unveiling the mysteries of attainment and of certainty; and which is the greatest science of Allah﷾ and the clearest way of Allah﷾ and the most manifest evidence of Allah﷾. The likeness of the light thereof is as a niche in which is a candle shining with radiance brighter than the dawn. It is the heart's Paradise, having fountains and boughs, one of them a fountain called Salsabil amongst the travellers on this Path; and in the view of the possessors of stations and graces, and it is best as a station and most excellent as a resting-place. There the righteous eat and drink, and there the free are gladdened and rejoiced; and like the Nile of Egypt it is a drink to them that endure patiently, but a grief to the people of Pharaoh and the unbelievers, even as Allah﷾ has said, "He lets many be misled thereby and He lets many be guided thereby" (Al-Quran 2:26). It is the cure for breasts, and the purge of sorrows, and the expounder of the Qur'an, and the abundance of gifts, and the cleansing of dispositions; by the hands of noble righteous scribes who forbid none shall touch it except the purified. Falsehood does not approach it either from before or behind, since Allah﷾

observes it and watches over it, and He is the best guardian and He is the most merciful of them that show mercy. And it has other titles of honour which Allah has bestowed upon it. We have confined ourselves to this little, for the little is an index to the much, and a mouthful is an index to the pool, and a handful is an index to a great threshing-floor.

The feeble slave who has need of the mercy of Allah most High, Muhammad son of Muhammad son of Al-Husayn of Balkh — may Allah accept from him says: "I have exerted myself to give length to the Poem in Rhymed Couplets, which comprises strange tales and rare sayings and excellent discourses and precious indications, and the path of the ascetics and the garden of the devotees -- brief in expression but manifold in meaning — at the request of my master and stay and support, the place of the spirit in my body, and the treasure of my to-day and my to-morrow, namely, the Shaykh, the exemplar for them that know God and the leader of them that possess right guidance and certainty, the helper of humankind, the trusted keeper of hearts and consciences, the charge deposited by Allah amongst His creatures, and His choice amongst His creation, and His injunctions to His Prophet and His secrets to His chosen one, the key of the treasuries of the empyrean, the trustee of the riches stored in the earth, the father of virtues, the Sword of the Truth and Religion, Hasan son of Muhammad son of al-Hasan, generally known as Ibn Akhi Turk, the Abu Yazid of the time, the Junayd of the age, the entirely veracious son of an entirely veracious sire and grandsire — may Allah be well-pleased with him and with them, a native of Urmiya, tracing his descent to the Shaykh who is honoured for having said, 'In the evening I was a Kurd, and in the morning I was an Arab.' May Allah﷾ sanctify his soul and the souls of his successors! How goodly is the ancestor and how goodly the successor! His is a lineage upon which the sun has cast its mantle, and a renown of ancestry before which the stars have dimmed their beams. Their courtyard has ever been Fortune's qibla, wherever the sons of the rulers turn, and Hope's Ka`ba which is circumambulated by deputations of the suitors for bounty. May it never cease to be thus, so long as a star rises and an orient sun appears above the horizon, to the end that it may be a fastness for the godly, spiritual, heavenly, super-celestial, illuminated ones who possess insight, the silent ones who behold, the absent ones who are present, the kings beneath threadbare garments, the nobles of the nations, the owners of excellences, the luminaries who display the evidences. Amen, O Lord of all created beings! And this is a prayer that will not be rejected, for it is a prayer that includes all classes of the creation. Glory be to Allah﷾, the Lord of all created beings, and Allah﷾ bless the best of His creatures, Prophetﷺ, and his kin, the noble, the pure!"

Prologue

Everyone who is left far from his source

Wishes back the time when he was united with it.

In every company I uttered my grieving cry;

I consorted with the unhappy and with them that rejoice.

Every one became my friend from his own opinion;

None sought out my secrets from within me.

My secret is not far from my complaint

But ear and eye lack the light.

Body is not veiled from soul, or soul from body

Yet none is permitted to see the soul.

The pain and suffering of another can only be understood through depth of perception and a richness of experience. Rumi talks about the anguish of the soul that is far removed from its reality which is its spiritual existence.

****

If our days are gone, let them go!—It is no matter.

Do You remain, for none is holy as You are!

Whoever is not a fish becomes sated with His water;

Whoever is without daily bread finds the day long.

None that is raw understands the state of the ripe:

Therefore my words must be brief. Farewell!
O son, burst your chains and be free!
How long will you be a bondsman to silver and gold?

Rumi describes three kinds of people.

First kind he compares to fish that can never get enough of the sea. Those that are spiritually awakened and are on a continuous journey of soaring to ever greater heights of spiritual awakening. He calls them ripe as they are "Complete" in their search for the Truth.

Then there are those who are not from the sea; they have been granted some part of awareness and they are content with that. They are "Deficient" in the understanding of the true purpose of life.

Third are the ones who have not been given any part of this spiritual awareness and theirs is a wasted life full of worldly pursuits. These are termed as raw and "Blocked" from the Truth.

Just like the "Blocked" cannot comprehend the state of the "Deficient", so a "Deficient" cannot understand the passion of the "Complete" in his search for the true purpose of life. Hence, Rumi says there is no point in trying to explain the passions of True Love of the Divine.

So then how does a "Deficient" rise to the height of a "Complete"?

Rumi answers that to rise spiritually and be able to embark on a life of true meaning it is incumbent upon man to break free from the chains of gold and silver, meaning material love. When this love will become weak, the love for Truth will become strong. That is the only way to live a life of purpose and to gain spiritual heights for which man was created.

It is important to note here that there are three kinds of relationships, other than that with Allah☀, which is the ultimate true connection that the soul desires.

1. Those that Religious Law has made compulsory, like parents, children, siblings, close of kin, community, etc. which are praiseworthy, and it is a sin to sever these.

2. Second are those which are prohibited; association with the opposite gender without legal relationship, ties with the unjust or evil-doers, etc. It is incumbent to leave them.

3. Lastly are those that are neither prohibited nor encouraged; passing acquaintances, friends, etc. There is no need to leave these but it is desirable to decrease engagement in them.

****

He whose garment is rent by a love
Is purged of covetousness and all defect.
Hail, O Love that bring us good gain —
You that art the physician of all our ills
The remedy of our pride and vainglory,
Our Plato and our Galen!
Through Love the earthly body soared to the skies:
The mountain began to dance and became nimble.
Love inspired Mount Sinai, O lover,
Sinai got drunk and *Moses fell in a swoon.*

True love (of Allah﷾) is explained as the supreme force that easily helps man cleanse his soul of greed, avarice, anger and all the negative thoughts and evil traits. Addressing this Love, Rumi says because of you, thoughts become noble and all spiritual diseases are healed. He compares it to a physician of the soul as it purges it and removes contempt and ego because Love demands humility of the spirit, as opposed to honour and glory which demand arrogance. Hence, both cannot flourish at the same time; if one is dominant the other has to leave. Rumi says Love is our Plato and Galen, helping us to cure the maladies of the soul.

Platonic love as devised by Plato concerns rising through levels of consciousness to wisdom and true beauty, from carnal attraction to individual bodies to attraction to souls, and eventually, union with the Truth. This is the ancient, philosophical interpretation. Platonic love is often contrasted with romantic, physical love.[xi]

Galen was a Greek physician, surgeon and philosopher in the Roman Empire. Galen's major works, On the Diagnosis and Cure of the Soul's Passion, discussed how to approach and treat psychological problems. This was Galen's early attempt at what would later be called psychotherapy. His book contained directions on how to provide counsel to those with psychological issues to prompt them to reveal their deepest passions and secrets, and eventually cure them of their mental deficiency.[xii]

The earthly body refers to Prophetﷺ when he travelled to the skies, the night of Mairaj (ascension) as mentioned in the Quran 17:1. The dancing of the mountain refers to Prophet Moosa's﷽

desire to see Allahﷻ (Quran 7:143). Prophet'sﷺ ascent to the sky was because of Love as the lover is granted closeness and loftiness. Moosa's request to see his Beloved was also because of his ardour and passion. Its manifestation resulted in the mountain coming into motion, whereas Moosa fell down unconscious.

Rumi intends to praise the power of love here.

Note: It is not possible to see Allahﷻ in this world (Quran 7:143).

There should be no confusion here because in spite of the manifestation Moosa fell unconscious and couldn't see.

Rumi is beseeching the Lord, who is our Helper, to help us to observe self-control in all circumstances, and explaining the harmful and pernicious consequences of indiscipline.

****

> **Were I joined to the lip of one in accord with me,**
> **I too, like the reed, would tell all that may be told;**
> **Whoever is parted from one who speaks his language**
> **Becomes dumb, though he have a hundred songs.**
> **When the rose is gone and the garden faded,**
> **You will hear no more the nightingale's story.**

After the discourse above on the glory of love and passion, the situation demanded that the effects and secrets of love should be explained in more detail; however, these are matters of interest and passion with depth in them. They cannot be explained to one who has not been initiated. There could be the danger of misunderstanding and transgression. Hence, Rumi excuses himself saying if he had the right recipient, he would surely have explained the mysteries of love like a true devotee.

Here Rumi explains the golden rule as a reason for the preceding verses, that a person may have lots of knowledge but if he does not find one who speaks his language or is on the same mental plane as he, then it is of no use.

The rose is the receiver of the nightingale's song, therefore in autumn there's no one to hear its song. Rumi says in the same way the correct listener is the true recipient of the subject; when such is not found silence is best.

****

The Beloved is all and the lover a veil;
The Beloved is living and the lover a dead thing.
When Love has no care for him, he is left
As a bird without wings. Alas for him then!
How should I have consciousness before or behind
When the light of my Beloved is not before me and behind?

Beloved is the Creator, the Only True Being and the lover is the creation, which only exists virtually. It has no existence beyond the Creator. For example, the Ruler asks the complainant if he registered a complaint with the police and the lawyer, to which he replies that the Ruler embodies the police and the lawyer. This, of course, doesn't mean the Ruler, police and lawyer are all one. It simply means that they are of no account as all authority and control rest with the Ruler.

Second line explains the principle that compared to a Perfect Being, imperfect is like non-existent. For example, there is a person who memorized certain chapters of the Quran, and so the villagers call him Hafiz (memorizer). However, there comes another person to live in the village who has memorized the whole Quran. Now when anyone enquires about a hafiz, people will point to the second person. The first will lose his status as hafiz when a perfect hafiz comes along. Or the governor will rule over the city till the king comes along. Then the governor will hand over the seat and ruling to the king.

In the same way, creation exists because the Creator gave them existence. The creation is weak and incomplete compared to the One Being, hence it is like non-existent in comparison. Rumi says to regard the One True Being, the Beloved, as living, whereas the creation is like the dead. They have a body but all authority is with the Creator.

This is the concept of Unity. A traveler on the path of spirituality has his focus on the One True Being. All other creation is like non-existent.

Al-Quran (28:88) Everything (that exists) will perish except His own Face. To Him belongs the Command, and to Him will you (all) be brought back.

Love is the force that joins the lover to the Beloved. When the lover focuses on the Beloved and has no inclination for anything else then the attention of the One True Being is attracted. Without this focus and magnetism the lover is like a bird without wings, helpless and powerless.

Without this care and appeal from the Beloved, the One True Being, there would be no security from the brigands and highwaymen on the path to spirituality, as mentioned about them in the Quran.

Al-Quran (7:16-17) (Satan) said, "Because you have put me in error, I shall surely sit in wait for them on your straight path. Then I will come to them from before them and from behind them and on their right and on their left. And You will not find most of them grateful (to You)."

The light of the Almighty engulfs the lover and protects from all sides.

Prophetﷺ said: O All\u0101h\ufdfb, place light in my heart, and on my tongue light, and in my ears light and in my sight light, and above me light, and below me light, and to my right light, and to my left light, and before me light and behind me light. Place in my soul light. Magnify for me light, and amplify for me light. Make for me light and make me a light. O All\u0101h\ufdfb, grant me light, and place light in my nerves and in my body light and in my blood light and in my hair light and in my skin light. All\u0101h\ufdfb, make for me a light in my grave... and a light in my bones.

****

Love wills that this Word should be shown forth:
If the mirror does not reflect, how is that?
Do you know why the mirror reflects nothing?
Because the rust is not cleared from its face.
O my friends listen to this tale:
In truth it is the very marrow of our inward state.

Rumi says love is limitless and its discourse has no end.

Al-Quran (18:109) Say: "If all the sea were ink for my Sustainer's words, the sea would indeed be exhausted before my Sustainer's words are exhausted! And [thus it would be] if we were to add to it sea upon sea."

However, it cannot be explained to one who has no clarity of vision as without it there can be no transformation and perception. If the mirror is covered with dust how can the image be clear? Rumi says the mirror of your heart is rusted with the love for the creation rather than the Creator. Hearts that are like the clear mirror filled with True Love are radiant with light and receptors of knowledge and perception.

This prologue to the Mathnavi is a summary of the total path to spirituality. It gives the beginning of the journey of the soul and provokes reflection for reawakening and restoration to the original state.

Story I

The King and the Handmaid

A king, while engaged on a hunting excursion, saw a beautiful maiden, and by promises of wealth and fortunes, induced her to accompany him. After a time she fell sick and the king had her treated by diverse physicians. As, however, they all omitted to say, "God be willing", their treatment was of no avail.

Al-Quran (18:23-24) and never say about anything, "Behold, I shall do this tomorrow", without adding, "if Allah so wills".

So the king fell down in prayer, and in answer to his sincere beseeching a physician was sent down from heaven. With a very skillful diagnosis he discovered that the real cause for the maiden's illness was her love for a certain goldsmith of Samarkand. In accordance with the physician's advice the goldsmith was fetched from Samarkand after heavy compensations in gold and silver, and married to the lovesick maiden. For six months the pair lived in utmost harmony and happiness. At the end of that period, the physician, by Divine command, gave the goldsmith a poisonous draught which caused his strength and beauty to decay. He then lost favour with the maiden, as her love for him was only superficial and based on desires of the self. Hence she was reunited with the king. This divine command was precisely similar to Allah's command to Abraham☐ to slay his son Ismail☐; and to the act of Khazir in slaying the boy, and is therefore, beyond human criticism.[xiii]

Al-Quran (37:102) And [one day,] when [the child Ismail] had become old enough to share in his [father Abraham's] endeavours, the latter said: "O my dear son! I have seen in a dream that I should sacrifice you: consider, then, what would be your view!" [Ismail] answered: "O my father! Do as you are commanded: you will find me, if Allah so wills, among those who are patient in adversity!"

Al-Quran (37:103) But as soon as the two (Abraham and Ismail) had surrendered themselves to [what they thought to be] the will of Allah, and [Abraham] had laid him (Ismail) down on his face…..(only relevant portion of verse quoted)

Al-Quran (18:74) And so the two (Khazir and Moosa☺) went on, till, when they met a young man, [the sage Khazir] slew him - (whereupon Moosa☺) exclaimed: "Have you slain an innocent human being without [his having taken] another man's life? Indeed, you have done a terrible thing!"

****

In olden time there was a king to whom belonged
The power temporal and also the power spiritual.
It chanced that one day he rode
With his courtiers to the chase.

On the king's highway the king espied a handmaiden:

The soul of the king was enthralled by her.

Forasmuch as the bird, his soul, was fluttering in its cage,

He gave money and bought the handmaiden.

After he had bought her and won to his desire,

By Divine destiny she sickened.

A certain man had an ass but no pack-saddle:

He got a saddle; the wolf carried away his ass.

He had a pitcher, but no water could be obtained:

When he found water, the pitcher broke.

The king gathered the physicians together from left and right

And said to them, "The life of us both is in your hands.

My life is of no account, she is the life of my life.

I am in pain and wounded: she is my remedy.

Whoever heals her that is my life will bear away with him

My treasure and pearls, large and small."

They all answered him, saying, "We will hazard our lives

And summon all our intelligence

and put it into the common stock.

Each one of us is the Messiah of a world:

In our hands is a medicine for every pain."

In their arrogance they did not say, "If God wills";

Therefore God showed unto them the weakness of Man.

I mean omission of the saving clause is a hardness of heart;

Not the mere saying of these words,

for that is a superficial circumstance.

How many a one has not pronounced the saving clause,

And yet his soul is in harmony with the soul of it!

The more cures and remedies they applied,
The more did the illness increase, and the need was not
fulfilled.

Rumi says this tale as it is in accordance with our own condition. Just as the king fell in love with the maiden in the same way the soul falls in love with the self and follows the demands of this love. As the maiden fell in love with the goldsmith, so the carnal self is engrossed with the worldly desires and passions. This creates dis-ease and affects the spiritual health of the soul enamoured by the carnal self. Rumi used the metaphor of king for the soul, maiden for the carnal self and the goldsmith for the worldly desires and lust. The king (soul) tried to get the maiden, his ailing self, treated by inept physicians, meaning untrained and inexperienced spiritual guides and there was no benefit. The divinely guided physician made the goldsmith (worldly desires and lust) ugly and unappealing to the maiden (self) and then killed it. In the same way a sincere and experienced spiritual guide separates the self from worldly desires and lust, so that it leaves them. It gains deliverance from these dis-eases of the mortal self and then the soul can benefit from this pure self.

The examples of the ass and the pitcher of water represent the flawed and deficient worldly life. Rumi is pointing out that it will never give complete satisfaction and there will always be one thing or the other amiss so don't get absorbed in it. The king got his desire, the handmaiden, but then she was of no use to him as she fell ill.

The two main topics of Rumi's writing are Oneness (Tauheed) and to follow the guidance of a sincere and experienced spiritual mentor (taqleed). The latter is difficult to find in this day and age, where all sorts of insincerity, worldly gains and vileness pollute the spiritual conditions.

****

When the king saw the powerlessness of those physicians,
He ran bare-footed to the mosque.
He entered the mosque and advanced to the mihrab
(niche for praying):
The prayer-carpet was bathed in the king's tears.
On coming to himself out of the flood of ecstasy
He opened his lips in goodly praise and reverence,
Saying, "O You whose least gift is the empire of the world,
What shall I say, inasmuch as You know the hidden thing?
O You with whom we always take refuge in our need,
Once again we have missed the way.
But You have said, 'Although I know your secret,
Nevertheless declare it forthwith in your outward act.'"
When from the depths of his soul he raised a cry,
The sea of Bounty began to surge.
Slumber overtook him in the midst of weeping.
He dreamed that an old man appeared
And said, "Good tidings, O king! Your prayers are granted.
If tomorrow a stranger comes for you, he is from me.

When he comes, he is the skilled physician.

Deem him authentic, for he is trusty and true.

In his remedy behold absolute magic.

In his temperament behold the power of Truth."

When the promised hour arrived and day broke

And the sun, from the east, began to burn the stars,

He saw a person excellent and worshipful,

A sun amidst a shadow,

Coming from afar, like the new moon.

He was non-existent, though existent in the form of

imagination.

In the countenance of the invisible guest was appearing

That imagination which the king beheld in his dream.

The king himself, instead of the chamberlains,

Went forward to meet his guest from the Invisible.

Both were seamen who had learned to swim,

The souls of both were knit together without sewing.

The king said, "You were my Beloved, not she;

But in this world deed issues from deed.

O you who art to me Mustafa, while I am like unto you `Umar

I will gird my loins to do you service."

Rumi says both were seamen who had learned to swim, meaning the king and the guest were both seekers of the spiritual path. Their souls were one in the search and love for Truth. Matters of the world are based on cause and effect. The king realized true love when he met a kindred spirit, but the love of the handmaiden (worldly passion) became the cause for this meeting.

Rumi uses the simile of Mustafa, Prophetﷺ as the master and his companion Umar r.a the servant. This tale is from ancient times, but the question of how the king knew about the Prophetﷺ does not arise as these are the words of Rumi, not the king.

****

Let us implore God to help us to deference and humility:
One who lacks self-control is deprived of the grace of the Lord.
The undisciplined man does not mistreat himself alone,
But he sets the whole world on fire.

Due to indiscipline this man causes harm to himself because he will suffer the consequences of his indiscipline. The world and the life in it are based on cause and effect. For every act there is an equal and opposite reaction. So whatever evil you do comes back to you and the good that you do stays with you. This is the cosmic law.

At the same time, he will cause harm to others in two ways.

One, in particular to those people, who see him living a life of selfish desires and uncontrolled evil, meet him and greet him warmly, but do not reproach him or stop him in any way possible. To allow evil and unfairness in spite of having the power to control it is a sin in itself. In these people greed and longing will also arise at the show of wealth and pomp.

Second, in general, to those who had no part in the injustice and evil, but suffer when calamities like drought, famine and plague befall a society due to the sins and transgressions of a few. These affect the good and the bad.

Al-Quran (8:25) And fear a trial which will not strike only those who have wronged among you exclusively; and know that Allah is severe in penalty.

Prophet said: When the people see a wrongdoer and do not prevent him, Allah will soon punish them all. Another version has: If acts of disobedience are done among any people who do not change them though they are able to do so, Allah will soon punish them all.

However, these trials are punishment from Allah for the evil-doers but a source of mercy for the innocent.

****

A table was coming down from heaven
Without headache and without selling and buying.
Some of the people of Moosa cried disrespectfully,
"Where is garlic and lentils?"
The heavenly bread and dishes were cut off:
There remained the toil of sowing and mattock and scythe.

Again, when Isa made intercession,

Allah sent food and bounty on trays,

But once more the insolent fellows omitted to show respect

And, like beggars, snatched away the food,

Isa entreated them, saying,

"This is lasting and will not fall from off the earth."

To show suspicion and greed

At the table of Majesty is ingratitude.

Because of those impudent wretches who were blinded by

greed,

That gate of mercy was closed upon them.

On account of withholding the poor-tax no rain-clouds arise,

And in consequence of fornication the plague spreads

in all directions.

Whatever befalls you of gloom and sorrow

Is the result of irreverence and lack of propriety nevertheless.

Any one behaving with irreverence in the path of the Friend

Is a brigand who robs men, and he is no man.

Through deference this Heaven has been filled with light,

And through discipline the angels became immaculate and holy.

By reason of propriety the sun was eclipsed,

And insolence caused an 'Azazil to be turned back from the

door.

The heaven is filled with the light of the sun, moon and stars because of their propriety and deference. When they were asked if they will follow their Lord's command willingly or by force, they said we come willingly.

Al-Quran (41:11) And He [it is who] said to them (mountains) and to the earth, "Come [into being], both of you, willingly or unwillingly!" - to which both responded, "We do come in obedience".

In the same way, the angels' decorum raised their status because when they were tested about the names of things they submitted to the Almighty and accepted their ignorance.

Al-Quran (2:32) They replied: "Limitless are You in Your glory! No knowledge have we save that which You have imparted unto us. Verily, You alone are all-knowing, truly wise."

Lack of respect in men, not the sun, is the reason of the eclipse. Some would argue that eclipse is due to the moon covering the sun, but that is the cause. However, due to His power of justice, when men commit all kinds of sin, Allah﷾ makes the sun dark to fill the hearts of men with fear.

Muhammadﷺ said: The sun and the moon are two of the signs of Allah﷾, with which He strikes fear into His slaves.

Azazil, the devil, was turned away from Heaven due to his arrogance and lack of respect.

✳✳✳✳✳✳✳✳✳

Being in love is made manifest by soreness of heart:
There is no sickness like heart-sickness.
The lover's ailment is separate from all other ailments:

Love is the astrolabe of the mysteries of God.
Whether love be from this side or from that side,
In the end it leads us beyond.

Love is intense and an ailment like no other because it consumes the body and soul. At the same time, love-sickness is different as other illnesses can be fatal but true love with Allahﷻ leads to immortality; and if it is a worldly love then the condition for immortality is that it leads to the true love of Allahﷻ.

Astrolabe is an instrument to measure the distance of the sun, etc. Rumi uses it metaphorically for love as an instrument to attain the hidden knowledge of God, which is not the case with other illnesses.

Rumi states that whether the love is for the creation or the Creator, it leads us to the true knowing and love of Allahﷻ. Any love of the creation which does not lead to the True Love is based on egoistic desires and cannot be called a source of access to the knowledge of God. However, the knowers of true love know how to transcend from the love of the creation to the love of the Creator.

Firstly, if one falls in love with the creation, then it is incumbent to restrain oneself, and not do anything that is against the moral injunctions because this would be contradictory to True Love.

Secondly, assume distance from the object of worldly love to avoid temptation which will result in breaking moral injunctions and hence, creating a distance from True Love.

Thirdly, contemplate and reflect that if this worldly creation is so beautiful then how must be the One who created it. This will shift the focus from the creation to the Creator.

Love is the desired state, whether permissible love for the creation or true love for the Creator. It develops softness of heart and enhanced sensitivity and pain. It empties the heart of all other thoughts and creates focus on the one who is desired. Then the only work left is to please the Creator by focusing this effort and striving for the sake of love toward Him through gratefulness and obedience.

Just like an engine which is warmed and moving, but in the wrong direction; rather than switch it off, all that needs to be done is to turn it in the right direction.

****

Whatever I say in exposition and explanation of Love,
When I come to Love I am ashamed of that.
Although the commentary of the tongue makes clear,
Yet silent love is clearer.
While the pen was making haste in writing,
It split upon itself as soon as it came to Love.
In expounding Love, the intellect lay down
like an ass in the mire:
It was Love that uttered the explanation of love
and being in love.

The proof of the sun is the sun:
If you require the proof, do not avert your face from Him!

Rumi says that I tried to explain the reality of love, but am now ashamed as I realize that love is a matter of feelings, sense and cognizance. Although reality of most things is clearer with words and description, but the reality of love is made clearer only by wordlessness. It is only through actual experience that the reality of love is manifest in the heart and then there is no need to understand it through another.

The pen is helpless in explaining love, as love is an experiential matter rather than theoretical. Here, Rumi uses the metaphor of a donkey that if it falls in the mire, it cannot go forth. Similarly, intellect is powerless to describe love; it is only love itself that when experienced, elucidates its reality. Love and being in love, both can only be explained through the experience of love itself.

Love is personified as the sun. There is no need of theory or explanation, just as the sun is its own proof, so is love the expounder of the reality of love. If the sun was explained with the intellect, it would be insufficient as its complete reality is evident only through our senses; so it is with love which is a sensual experience and can never be fully explained through intellect. If you want to understand it fully, don't search for other ways to find its true meaning. Turn your heart and soul to the Almighty. You will find the light of True Love enter your being and fill you with ecstasy. It will guide you to the real meaning of life.

****

When a thorn darts into any one's foot,
He sets his foot upon his knee,
And keeps searching for its head with the point of a needle,
And if he does not find it, he keeps moistening it with his lip.
A thorn in the foot is so hard to find:
How is it with a thorn in the heart? Answer!
If every low fellow had seen the thorn in the heart,
When would sorrows gain the upper hand over any one?
Somebody sticks a thorn under a donkey's tail:
The donkey does not know how to get rid of it: he starts jumping.
He jumps, and the thorn sinks deeper:
It needs an intelligent person to extract a thorn.
In order to get rid of the thorn,
the donkey from irritation and pain
Went on kicking and dealing blows in a hundred places.

Rumi says that when a simple problem like a thorn getting stuck in the foot has to be dealt with so much care and concern, and takes so much effort, then how can a thorn (pain or worry) in the heart be easy to find and cure. If every person, unskilled in spiritual and psychological treatment, could resolve the issues of the heart then there would be no problems to solve. Every human would be free of worry and distress. Hence, it is imperative to seek counsel from the skilled mentor and guide, who is also wise spiritually to find an answer to the troubles of the heart. Then he gives the example of a donkey and how it only hurts itself more and more in order to relieve itself of the pain from the thorn since it has no understanding of the cure. This metaphor explains the significance of seeking guidance and counsel for the ailments of the heart and mind from the skilled. Trying to treat them through the unskilled or by one's self will only increase the agony of the soul.

****

When your heart becomes the grave of your secret,
Then your desire will be gained more quickly.
The Prophetﷺ said that anyone who hides his inmost thought
Will soon attain the object of his desire.
When seeds are hidden in the earth,
Their inward secret becomes the lush greenery of the garden.
If gold and silver were not hidden,
How would they get nourishment in the mine?

Rumi is advising the reader to keep his affairs secret and only reveal to the one who is wise and trustworthy. He says not to share matters of the heart and mind to all and sundry, but to a faithful mentor skilled in counsel and understanding. He gives two examples to explain his point.

One is of the seed as it only grows into a blooming plant after being hidden and nourished under the earth for a specified time.

The other example is of gold and silver as they are buried in the mines for countless years where they gain their brilliance. If they were removed before time, they would be mere rocks.

****

There are true promises, comforting to the heart;
There are false promises, filled with anxiety.
The promise of the noble is current coin;
The promise of the unworthy becomes anguish of the soul.

Rumi talks about promises made by the honest and the dishonest. True promises create peace and tranquility in the heart, whereas the promises of the insincere create confusion and uneasiness of the heart.

Messenger of Allah said: Give up what is doubtful to you for that which is not doubtful; for truth is peace of mind and falsehood is doubt.

The pledge and assurance of a sincere spiritual mentor is a source of contentment and peace for the heart whether it is to educate or give glad tidings of the fruit of labour. An inept or insincere person's pledge only creates anxiety in the heart because the purpose of such a promise is only for the sake of treachery or falsehood. Promises should be fulfilled otherwise the reputation will be tainted and people's trust will be lost. Those who honour their commitments will see the rewards in this world and the next.

****

<u>After the Handmaid and the Goldsmith had spent six months of love and harmony:</u>

Thereafter the physician prepared for the goldsmith a potion,

So that when he drank it he began to dwindle away before her.

When because of sickness his beauty remained not,

The soul of the girl remained not in his influence.

Since he became ugly and ill-favoured and sallow-cheeked,

Little by little he became cold in her heart.

Those loves which are for the sake of colour are not love:

In the end they are a disgrace.

Would that he too had been disgrace altogether

So that that evil judgment might not have come to pass upon him!

After the goldsmith and the maiden had spent six months of love and joy together the physician gave him a potion that made his body weak and sickened his core. As he lost his beauty and strength, the maiden's love for him also dwindled and decreased, until she didn't care for him anymore.

Rumi explains a basic principle that love for the sake of external beauty and gratification of selfish desires is not true love at all. It only leads to sorrow and regret.

The maiden's love was only virtual and not true, otherwise, there was the fear that with the goldsmith's dying there would be danger of her ending her life too, as in the case of many tales of love like Romeo and Juliet, etc. In such a case, the physician would have not resorted to his scheme. Love of the creation for the mere gratification of ego is undesirable, and even more so when it is so harmful to the other. Rumi says to then consider how hazardous such a love must be to the self.

****

Although the wall casts a long shadow,
The shadow turns back again towards it.
This world is the mountain, and our actions the shout:
The echo of the shouts comes to us."

Every action has an equal and opposite reaction. The good or the bad, whatever a person does will come back to him just like the shadow returns to the wall and the echo comes back to the one who shouted. Rumi likens the world as a mountain and our actions as the shout that comes back to us in the form of the echo. We should be mindful of the consequences of our deeds.

****

The peacock's plumage is its enemy:
O many the king who has been slain by his magnificence!
He said, "I am the musk deer on account of whose gland
That hunter shed my pure blood.
Oh, I am the fox of the field
Whose head they stealthily cut off for the sake of the fur.

Oh, I am the elephant whose blood was shed
By the blow of the mahout for the sake of the bone.
He who has slain me for that which is other than I
Does not know that my blood does not sleep.
To-day it lays on me and to-morrow it lies on him:
When does the blood of one such as I am, go to waste like this?

This is the goldsmith's cry as he is slowly losing his life due the physician's poison.

****

The love of the dead is not enduring,
Because the dead one is never coming to us.
Love of the Living One is every moment fresher
Than a bud in the spirit and in the sight.
Choose the love of that Living One who is Everlasting,
Who gives you to drink of the wine that increases life.
Choose the love of Him from Whose love
All the prophets gained power and glory.
Do not say, "We have no admission to that King."
Dealings with the generous are not difficult.

Love of the creation will one day end, by death or by distance, but the love of the Creator is the true love. It is everlasting. His love is like the refreshing wine and a nourishing drink through which He gives you a taste of His enduring love. This True Love gave the Prophets⸎ power and glory as no other mortal souls could ever reach.

Rumi says that do not think it's impossible to reach the High and Mighty. If you cannot gain access to Him through your own efforts, then He, through His infinite mercy and generosity will pull you towards His court.

Messenger of Allahﷺ said: Allahﷻ says: 'I am just as My slave thinks of Me when he remembers Me.' By Allahﷻ! Allahﷻ is more pleased with the repentance of His slave than one of you who unexpectedly finds in the desert his lost camel. Allahﷻ says: 'He who comes closer to Me one span, I come closer to him a cubit; and he who comes closer to Me a cubit, I come closer to him a fathom; and if he comes to Me walking, I come to him running'.

✳✳✳✳✳✳✳✳✳

The slaying of this man by the hand of the physician

Was not on account of hope or fear.

He did not slay him to humour the king,

Until the Divine command and inspiration came.

As for the boy whose throat was cut by khazir/Khadir,

The vulgar do not comprehend the mystery thereof.

He that receives from God inspiration and answer,

Whatsoever He may command is the essence of right.

If One who bestows life should slay, it is allowable.

He is the vicegerent, and his hand is the hand of God.

This refers to a story in the eighteenth chapter of the Quran. There is a description of some supernatural being who comes and interacts with Prophet Moosa☺.

Prophet Moosa☺ had asked Allah☺ to guide him to somebody who's more knowledgeable than him. So, with Allah's☺ counsel he meets this wiser individual, Khazir/Khadir? and agrees to travel with this individual on condition that he [Prophet Moosa☺] will not question anything this person does.

They come to a boy whom Khazir/Khadir kills and Prophet Moosa ☺ protests about why he killed an innocent boy. He said remember you're not to ask me about what I do until I volunteer to explain it to you. Eventually he explains that this boy belonged to righteous parents. By Divine knowledge Khazir learns that he will turn out to be aggressive against his parents and was commanded to replace him with one that would be better towards the parents.

So, there was wisdom behind this activity obviously guided by Divine inspiration and not by human knowledge.

And this is where the difference lies between the action of Khazir and somebody else who, a human being, may take the life of another, as they describe it, for the purpose of "honor killing" etc. This is dishonorable murder. It is wrong. We don't have Allah's☺ explicit knowledge to guide us factually and absolutely know what is the best course of action in the situation. But we have his instructions telling us not to take human life. So, Allah☺ can send His angels or other inspired being to do what He commands them to do. As in this case the taking of the life of a child.

****

Like Ismail, lay your head before him.
Gladly and laughingly give up your soul before his dagger,
In order that your soul may remain laughing until eternity,
Like the pure soul of Ahmad (Prophetﷺ) with the One.

Prophet Ismailﷻ is the figure known in Judaism, Christianity, and Islam as Prophet Abraham's ﷻ son, born to Bibi Hagarﷻ (Hajar or Hajarah). Prophet Ismailﷻ is regarded as a Prophet and an ancestor to the last Prophet Mohammedﷺ, referred to as Ahmad here. Prophet Ibrahimﷻ was ordered to sacrifice Ismail A.S. to which he readily agreed as it was a Divine command. However, Allahﷻ saved Ismail who also became associated with his father Ibrahim with Makkah and the construction of the Kaaba, the holy house of Allahﷻ.

****

Lovers drain the cup of joy at the moment
When the fair ones slay them with their own hands.
The king did not commit that bloodshed because of lust:
Cease from thinking evil and disputing.
You thought that he committed a foul crime.

In purity how should the sublimation leave alloy?

The purpose of this discipline and this rough treatment

Is that the furnace may extract the dross from the silver.

The testing of good and bad is in order

That the gold may boil and bring the scum to the top.

If his act were not the inspiration of God,

He would have been a dog that rends, not a king.

He was unstained by lust and covetousness and passion.

He did justly, but good that wore the aspect of evil.

If Khazir damaged the boat in the sea,

In Khazir's damaging there are a hundred moralities.

The imagination of Moses, notwithstanding

his illumination and excellence,

Was screened from that. Do not fly without wings!

That is a red rose; do not call it blood.

He is intoxicated with Reason; do not call him a madman.

Had it been his desire to shed the blood of a Moslem,

I am an infidel if I would have mentioned his name.

The highest heaven trembles at praise of the wicked,

And by praise of him the devout man is moved to think evil.

He was a king and a very heedful king;

He was elect and the elect of God.

One who is slain by a King like this,

He leads him to fortune and to the best estate.

Unless He had seen advantage to him in doing violence to him,

How should that absolute Mercy have sought to do violence?

The child trembles at the barber's scalpel

The fond mother is happy in that pain.

He takes half a life and gives a hundred lives:

He gives that which enters not into your imagination.
You are judging from yourself,
But you have fallen far, far. Consider well!

All the tests and trials of this life, whether worldly or spiritually, are to remove vices and purge the soul so it can reach loftier stations. Silver and gold have to be heated at highest of temperatures to bring out the scum so that their glitter shines forth.

Al-Quran (10:36) And most of them follow not except assumptions. Indeed, assumption avails not against truth at all. Indeed, Allah is knowing of what they do.

Story II

The Oilman and his Parrot

An oilman possessed a parrot which used to amuse him with its agreeable prattle, and watched his shop when he went out. One day, when the parrot was alone in the shop, he upset one of the oil jars by mistake. When the oilman returned home he thought the parrot had done it in mischief. In his anger he struck the parrot such a blow on the head that all his feathers dropped off. The parrot was so stunned it lost the power of speech. One day, the parrot saw a bald-headed ascetic passing the shop. Recovering his speech, it cried out, "Hey, whose oil jar did you upset?" The passers-by smiled at the parrot's innocence in mistaking baldness caused by age, choice or distinction with the loss of his own feathers due to the blow.

The moral of this story is that it's a folly to compare the actions of the worldly to that of the holy and spiritually awakened, though outwardly they may resemble and seem the same. Just as the parrot compared his own baldness to the holy man's, and generalized that he too, like the parrot, was beaten up by his master. The parrot became a laughing stock for his ridiculous comparison.[xiv]

****

There was a green grocer who had a parrot,

A sweet-voiced green talking parrot.

On the bench, it would watch over the shop

And talk finely to all the traders.

In addressing human beings it would speak;

It was skilled in the song of parrots.

It sprang from the bench and flew away

And spilled the bottles of rose-oil.

Its master came from the direction of his house

And seated himself on the bench at his ease as a merchant

does.

He saw the bench was full of oil and his clothes greasy;

He struck the parrot on the head: it was made bald by the blow.

For some few days it refrained from speech.

The greengrocer, in repentance, heaved deep sighs,

Tearing his beard and saying,

"Alas! The sun of my prosperity has gone under the clouds.

Would that my hand had been broken at that moment!

How did I strike on the head of that sweet-tongued one?"

He was giving presents to every ascetic,

That he might get back the speech of his bird.

After three days and three nights, he was seated on the bench,

Distraught and sorrowful, like a man in despair,

Showing the bird every sort of marvel

That maybe it would begin to speak.

Meanwhile a bald ascetic, clad in a coarse woollen frock,

Passed by, with a head hairless as the outside of bowl and

basin.

Then the parrot began to talk,

Screeched at the ascetic and said, "Hey, fellow!

How were you mixed up with the bald, O bald one?

Did you, then, spill oil from the bottle?"

The bystanders laughed at the parrot's inference,

Because it deemed the wearer of the frock to be like itself.

Do not measure the actions of holy men by yourself,

Though sher (lion) and shir (milk) are similar in writing.

On this account the whole world is gone astray.

Scarcely any one knows of God's Abdals.

They set up equality with the prophets;

They supposed the saints to be like themselves.

"Behold," they said, "We are men, they are men;

Both we and they are in bondage to sleep and food."

In blindness they did not perceive

That there is an infinite difference between.

Rumi states that the shallow and superficial are deprived of insight. They are like the blind, but of the soul, though they may have sight of the eye. They cannot recognize the difference between Abdal (saint) and ordinary human beings like themselves.

Abdal" is the plural of "Badal" or rather "Badeel", and means "those who get replaced", "those who serve as a partial replacement to the role of the prophets" or "friends of God". The Abdal are the group of true, pure believers in God. They serve God during their lifetime; when they die, they are immediately replaced by another selected by God from a larger group said to be the 500 "Akhyar", i.e., the semi-divine good ones. The Abdal are headed by their leader, "Al-Ghawth" ("the Helper"), who is said to reside in Mecca. This leader is often referred to as the Qutb, which means "Pole" in Arabic. This leader though unknown to the public is usually sought out by all of the lower ranking members of the Abdal.[xv]

The missions of the Abdal are to be God's merciful subjects everywhere they reside and to render the helping, blessing hand to all of God's creatures.

They have divine powers and super-natural abilities. A person does not recognize that he is one of the Abdal until he becomes aware of his status suddenly though a revelation. It is said that Abdal can be identified through their continuous good deeds and forgiving nature. They may be rich or poor, married or bachelor, child or adult. Such concepts are established in the Sunni branch of Islam, and in particular in the latter's original Sufi schools of spiritual disciplines.

The Abdal function as the keepers of equilibrium in the world and preserve it between the times when prophets are present. Varying in classification and denomination, the identity of the Abdal are entirely unknown to the public and even to themselves. With the ability to transmit blessings (baraka) and perform miracles (karāmāt) the Abdal as a whole are able to adequately fill the role of prophet. Similarly, it is believed that when judgement day comes, they will act as intermediaries between God and the human race.[xvi]

In the same way, they regarded the Prophets sent by Allahﷻ as themselves. Even though physical characteristics might be similar, but spiritually, they are above and beyond the capacity of ordinary people.

Al-Quran (14:10) Said the apostles sent unto them: "Can there be any doubt about [the existence and oneness of] Allah, the Originator of the heavens and the earth? It is He who calls unto you, so that He may forgive you [whatever is past] of your sins and grant you respite until a term [set by Him is fulfilled]." [But] they replied: "You are nothing but mortal men like ourselves! You want to turn us away from what our forefathers worshiped: well, then, bring us a clear proof [of your being Allah's message-bearers]!"

****

Both species of bee ate and drank from the place,
But from that one came a sting, and from this other honey.
Both species of deer ate grass and drank water:
From this one came dung, and from that one pure musk.
Both reeds drank from the same water-source,
This one is empty and that one sugar.
Consider hundreds of thousands of such likenesses and observe
That the distance between the two is a seventy years' journey.
Just because certain actions are similar between any two
Does not remove the huge distance of status
and worth between them.
This one eats, and filth is discharged from him;

That one eats, and becomes entirely the light of God.

This one eats, is born nothing but avarice and envy;

That one eats, is born nothing but love of the One.

This one is good soil and that one brackish and bad;

This one is a fair angel and that one a devil and wild beast.

If both resemble each other in aspect, it may well be:

Bitter water and sweet water have clearness.

Who knows except a man possessed of taste?

He knows the sweet water from the brine.

Rumi defines the difference between the noble and the disgraced. Both eat the same food but the noble soul lights up the world with his actions of generosity, kindness and piety, whereas the disgraced only makes the world a soiled, unhappy place to live with his meanness, dishonesty and treachery.

A man who has a clear soul and a light within his breast is like one whose sense of taste is strong and can make out the difference between bitter and sweet water. Both waters have similarities like fluidity and clarity but differ vastly in quality and taste.

✳✳✳✳✳✳✳✳✳

Comparing magic with miracle,

He fancies that both are founded on deceit.

The magicians of Prophet Moosa,

For contention's sake, lifted up a rod like his.

Between this rod and that rod there is a vast difference;

From this action to that action is a great way.

This action is followed by the curse of God

That action receives in payment the mercy of God.

Rumi shows the difference between sight, which is a physical attribute of the human body, and insight, which is a spiritual attribute in the one with a pure soul.

When Pharoah's magicians competed with Prophet Moosa and brought staffs like him their's changed to snakes and so did Prophet Moosa's. Even though both the actions and reactions were same but one that was magic was damned. The other that was from Moosa was blessed by the will of Allah.

Al-Quran (7:109) The great ones among Pharaoh's people said: "Verily, this is indeed a sorcerer of great knowledge."

This refers to the perception of the Pharoah in the event mentioned in the Quran, as he saw both, the actions of Prophet Moosa and the magicians as same, acts of magic. However, there was a deep difference between the two actions. The magicians' act was based on magic and had the curse of Allah on it. Prophet Moosa's act was blessed by Allah as it was based on His command.

Al-Quran (7:117) And [then] We inspired Moosa, "Throw down your staff!" - and lo! it swallowed up all their deceptions.

****

The infidels in competing have the nature of an ape:
The nature is a cancer within the breast.
Whatever a man does, the ape at every moment
Does the same thing that he sees done by the man.
He thinks, "I have acted like him".
How should that quarrelsome-looking one know the difference?
This one acts by the Command,
and he for the sake of quarrelling.
Pour dust on the heads of those who have quarrelsome faces!

Rumi defines the actions of the soul guided by the light of Allahﷻ and those guided by worldly or selfish motives. When the heart is tainted by deception and dishonor it loses insight and depth of perception. Nothing is gained by copying another for the sake of meanness and competition. Just like a monkey copies the actions of a man and thinks it's equal to man, but cannot discern the difference between the two acts. Man's action is governed by morality, thought processes and critical thinking, for worldly or spiritual benefits, either according to the command of Allahﷻ or against it.

There is no conscious thought or reflection in the monkey's imitation of a man's actions; his only purpose is mindlessly copying man. Obnoxious and evil disposition can never be the same as benign and reflective. Even though their actions may seem the same to the undiscerning eye but there is a vast difference in their purpose and reality.

****

That hypocrite joins in ritual prayer with the conformist

For quarrelling's sake, not for supplication.

In prayer and fasting and pilgrimage and alms-giving

The true believers are with the hypocrite in victory and defeat.

Victory in the end is to the true believers;

Upon the hypocrite defeat in the state hereafter.

Although both are intent on one game, in relation to each other

They are the man of Merv and the man of Rayy.

Each one goes to his abiding-place;

Each one fares according to his name.

If he be called a true believer, his soul rejoices;

And if you say "hypocrite," he becomes filled with fire.

His name is loved on account of its essence;

This one's name is loathed on account of its harmful qualities.

Mim and waw and mim and nun do not confer honour:

The word momin is only for the sake of definition.

If you call him hypocrite,

This vile name is stinging within like a scorpion.

If this name is not derived from Hell,

Then why is there the taste of Hell in it?

The foulness of that ill name is not from the letters;

The bitterness of that sea-water is not from the vessel.

The letters are the vessel: therein the meaning is like water;

The sea of the meaning is with Him in the Ummu 'l-Kitab.

In this world the bitter sea and the sweet sea —

Between them is a barrier which they do not seek to cross.

Know that both these flow from one origin.
Pass on from them both, go to their origin!

Rumi compares the hypocrite to the true believer (momin). They are as different as one from Khorasan (man of Merv), towards the east and one from Iraq (man of Ray), towards the west. Though both exhibit the same actions but their destinations are as far from each other as east and west. The hypocrite's final abode is hell, whereas the believer's heaven. Each will be dealt with as the Almighty has named them, because their names not only represent them outwardly, but also their reality.

A combination of alphabets only convey the title; the meaning is in the quality of the one who is named. Momin (believer) and munafiq (hypocrite) represent the attributes that each possesses and the qualities of honour or evil found within their self.

Mim, waw and nun are merely letters of the Arabic alphabet used for the distinction of the one addressed with the combination of these words which is momin. They don't contain eminence and dignity in themselves, but represent the qualities of the one addressed by this name.

In the same way, the word hypocrite sounds so obnoxious because it is derived from the immoral and evil qualities that lead to hell.

Rumi, as is his style, very easily slips into the topic of Tauheed (Oneness of Allahﷻ) as that is near and dear to his heart and dominant to his fancy. He uses the metaphor of sea for Allahﷻ.

Just like the sea is the source of water for rivers and lakes which through the process of the water cycle returns back to the sea, He is the source of all things and all things return to Him. The bitter sea represents the vile disposition and the sweet sea, the noble disposition. At times, it's hard to distinguish the difference between the two. For example, the difference between generosity and extravagance, stinginess and prudence, anger for the sake of Allah and anger for the sake of ego, humility and subservience, arrogance and courage. All these qualities seem very similar but there is a curtain that separates them and doesn't let them get mixed up. This distinction is in the worth and effect of each quality. Generosity has the spirit for granting maximum benefit to others, whereas extravagance is spending for self-gratification. Even though both represent excess spending but this distinguishes the difference between them.

Hence, these verses repeat the earlier topic, that things might seem similar on the surface so do not be misled. Rumi once again returns to the theme of Oneness and says that both these seas, bitter and sweet, originate from one Source. Don't get fixated on them and the worldly pleasures; pass them by and search for the True One.

****

Without the touchstone you will never know
In the evaluation impure gold and fine gold by judgment.
Anyone in whose soul God shall put the touchstone,

He will distinguish certainty from doubt.

A piece of rubbish jumps into the mouth of a living man,

And only when he ejects it is he at ease.

When, amongst thousands of morsels,

one little piece of rubbish entered,

The living man's sense tracked it down.

The worldly sense is the ladder to this world;

The spiritual sense is the ladder to Heaven.

Seek the well-being of the former sense from the physician;

Beg the well-being of the latter sense from the Beloved.

The health of the former arises from

the flourishing state of the body;

The health of the latter arises from the ruin of the body.

Real and artificial gold seem the same to the naked eye, and would need to be tested through the touchstone to identify the genuine gold. Similarly vile and pure dispositions seem similar to the naked eye, and need the glow of insight to discern the difference. Those whom Allahﷻ grants this light of perception can distinguish between doubt, an effect of the vile disposition and certainty of Truth which is acquired through an honorable disposition.

Messenger of Allahﷺ said: Ask your heart regarding it. Piety is that which contents the soul and comforts the heart and sin is that which causes doubts and perturbs the heart, even if people pronounce it lawful and give you verdicts on such matters again and again.

This saying is only for those who honor and maintain their covenant with Allahﷻ and are obedient to their Lord. They are granted the glow of insight and purity of heart, which gives them trust in this respect. Just like a man with a healthy sense of taste can discern the rubbish that enters his mouth along with the food, so the one gifted with insight can identify the evil from the pure.

In the previous verses, Rumi talked about the senses as a way to gain knowledge and understanding; these verses are the completion of this topic. Through the physical/ superficial senses we gain knowledge of the world and through the virtuous/pure/moral senses we gain spiritual knowledge. If you want to be treated for your bodily senses, then go to a doctor, but for spiritual health and growth, go to a qualified and sincere mentor/spiritual guide. Physical health is gained by fixing the body and nurturing it. Spiritual health is gained by restraint, self-control, sabotaging the physical needs and denying the body.

Rumi says gain the light of knowledge through effort and restraining worldly passions and lusts. This will grant the noor (light) of true knowledge which will help to distinguish between good and bad, the common and the special.

****

The spiritual way ruins the body and,
After having ruined it, restores it to prosperity.

Ruined the house for the sake of the golden treasure,

And with that same treasure built it better.

Cuts off the water and cleanses the river-bed,

Then causes drinking water to flow in the river-bed.

Cut the skin and drew out the iron point—

Then fresh skin grew over it.

Attacked the fortress and took it from the infidel,

Then reared there on a hundred towers and ramparts.

Rumi gives hope and courage to the one walking the path of spirituality. He compares spiritual and physical health. Physical health is acquired through developing the body by eating, sleeping, enjoying company, fulfilling its needs, exercising, etc. Spiritual health is acquired when bodily needs are denied through minimizing eating, sleeping, and all other desires of the flesh. After going through the discipline of spiritual exercises, the destruction of the bodily desires will lead to immortality of the soul. This is the fruit of this labour. The One who owns the soul (Allahﷻ) will first annihilate the bodily passions through devotional exercises that the sincere spiritual guide will suggest according to His commands. Then He will restore it through spiritual life which will also purify the body and give it a meaningful existence. The boons of Jannah and the nearness of Allahﷻ are achieved through piety, which is acquired through a body cleansed of lust and selfish desires. The righteous believe they will be raised on the Day of Judgement with this very body. Rumi gives four examples to show how destroying the ego and bodily desires leads to a superior existence.

- A person digs up his house when he finds that there is treasure buried under it and then rebuilds an even finer house with his wealth.

- A river bed is made dry by cutting off its water, only to clean it and then let the clear water flow abundantly.

- A spear pierces a man's body and its metal gets lodged in it causing poison. It will have to be cut to take out the metal, even though there will be pain and damage to the skin. However, afterwards fresh, healthy new skin will grow back.

- The fortress is conquered from the enemy after constant attack to destroy its structure with canon and mortar, so the victorious army can enter and capture them. This demolishes the walls and parapets. However, after the victory the fortress is rebuilt stronger and better than before.

All these examples show that the denial of the body heals it of debasement and corruption and leads to the replenishment of the soul. Hence, the wise should not lose heart, but, in fact, accept it and bear it.

Here, it is important to understand two important points:

One: The benefits of the self are of two kinds; its rights and its resources. Therefore, in the struggle and austerity to gain spirituality, the resources are denied or decreased but the rights of the self are not wasted as this is against the command of Allah.

Allah's Messenger said: Your body has a right over you...........

This denial of the rights of the body damages the soul too. It leads to weakness, affects the health and makes one incapable of attending to the obligatory prayers and duties; this curtails spiritual progress.

Two: The struggle and austerity prescribed by the righteous elders to shun the desires of the body is only as a treatment, just like a person suffering from some bodily ailment is asked to refrain from certain foods, etc. This is not to be regarded as worship or a way to gain nearness to Allah﷾. Hence, this is not to be considered innovation in religion.

Al-Quran (5:87) O You who have attained to faith! Do not deprive yourselves of the good things of life which God has made lawful to you……" (only relevant portion of verse quoted)

It is an innovation only if this denial of bodily needs is taken as a source of worship and nearness to Him. The purpose of the pious elders was only that as excessive indulgence in desires leads to the animalistic qualities like ego, lust, etc., it creates apathy and negligence in service and duties. At times these desires of the self are abandoned due to the dominance of the love of Allah﷾ as there is no inclination towards these desires. Hence it is not Sunnah nor innovation (bidah).

****

Who shall describe the action of Him who has no like?
This that I have said necessity is providing.

> **Sometimes it appears like this**
> **and sometimes the contrary of this.**
> **The work of religion is nothing but bewilderment.**
> **Not one bewildered in such a way**
> **that his back is towards Him; no, but**
> **One bewildered like this and drowned**
> **and intoxicated with the Beloved.**
> **The face of the one is set towards the Beloved;**
> **The face of the other is just his own face.**

After explaining the way to attain spirituality and the nearness of the Beloved Allahﷻ, Rumi goes on to explain that even though we try through different efforts and denial of the self to reach that state, some may reach it without any effort. Affairs of religion are perplexing and mysterious.

First there is endeavor and passion to find the True Beloved, and then attainment to knowing and nearness. **This is called the path of performance/effort.** However, sometimes the state of love and spirituality is attained first and then the passion and desire to worship and to struggle on the path of True Love. **This is called the path of absorption.** This could be caused by the companionship of a pious mentor, or reading of certain narrative/anecdote, or for no reason in particular. The seeker is completely absorbed in his struggle to attain knowing and awareness of the One True Beloved after being drawn onto the path.

This what Cal Newport says in his book "So Good They Can't Ignore You": You don't follow your passion – passion follows you as you work to gain excellence. Of course, he talks in the context of career and work.

Hence, who can determine or define the work of Allah﷾. When the seeker sees this and perceives his own internal and external affairs, he is filled with astonishment and wonder. Surprise and wonder is not caused only because of unawareness. At times, in spite of knowing, the qualified, pious elder is taken by surprise because there is never complete knowing and every mystery brings awe and wonderment.

However, this surprise and bewilderment is not in affairs of the essential doctrines of Islam like obligatory prayer, fasting, etc. as attainment of these is compulsory. Here only the inner matters of the heart are being referred to.

Hence, wonderment is of two kinds; one due to ignorance and this is undesirable and disreputable. The second is in spite of excessive knowledge and manifestation, because of the lack of complete realization of the Truth. This is desirable and honourable.

The true believer and gnostic is in a perpetual state of wonder, but his amazement and wonder is not like the one who has his back towards his Friend, meaning in a state of abandonment and neglect towards Allah﷾. In fact, his awe is because he is submerged and deeply engrossed in the study of spirituality and the search for Allah﷾. This is desirable wonderment.

Then Rumi explains that desirable wonderment is of two kinds; one where the believer's focus is on the Friend (Allahﷻ) and the second where the focus is itself the focus of the Friend. This means some are absorbed to the extent that they are aware of their own selves, and cognizant to their own being, whereas some lose all sense of self and their focus and intent is nonexistent. They are in a state of intoxication and lose themselves in the Truth. This is the loftiest state of the human soul.

****

Since there is many a devil that has the face of Adam,

It is not well to give your hand to every hand.

Because the fowler produces a whistling sound

In order to decoy the bird.

The bird may hear the note of its kindred

And come down from the air and find trap and knife-point.

The vile man will steal the language of ascetics,

That he may thereby chant a spell over one who is simple.

The work of men is light and heat;

The work of vile is trickery and shamelessness.

They make a woollen lion for the purpose of begging;

They give the title of Ahmad to Bu Musaylim;

To Bu Musaylim remained the title

of Kadhdhab (Great Liar),

To Mohammed remained Ulu 'l-albab.

The wine of God, its seal is pure musk,

As for wine, its seal is stench and torment.

Rumi explains about two kinds of devils; of men and demons (jinns). Hence, practice caution in making an allegiance with anyone who claims to be a spiritual mentor without proper investigation. For example the hunter uses the sound of the animal he hunts to trap it. The animal hears the sound of its kind/breed, comes out and falls into the trap. Similarly, the cunning and vile, for worldly benefits, copy the sayings and manners of the pious to cheat the simple minded who become indoctrinated and fall into loss and misguidance.

By light, is meant the light of faith and knowledge; by heat, the heat of Divine Love. This indicates the qualities of a qualified spiritual mentor, that is, knowledge of Truth and True Love, whereas a deceiver has fraud and unfaithfulness.

Rumi has summarized the definition of the sincere spiritual guide. Hazrat Thanvi☐ explains in more detail that for bodily ailments a doctor is needed who is both healthy and can treat others, as the principal is "Opinion of the unfit is unfit". Similarly, for diseases of the soul a qualified guide is needed who is God-fearing and pious, while at the same time is an effective counsellor and mentor for others to develop their spirituality. A mentor with poor faith and ineffective spiritual practices cannot be relied upon to be sincere in guidance as he himself is misguided. Moreover, he will not have the noor (light) of Truth to groom and educate his disciple. At the same time, if he is God-fearing and pious but does not have understanding of how to educate and guide spiritually, then he too can't fulfill the needs of the Seeker of the True Path. A physician's authenticity is gauged by the fact that he has studied medical sciences and received certification, then interned with a qualified practitioner, has sensible clients and people are cured by him. Similarly, a spiritual guide must have spent considerable years in the internship of a qualified, pious elder, people of knowledge and understanding have a good opinion of him, his companionship increases True Love (of Allahﷻ) and decreases worldly lust, and the condition of people near him shows constant improvement. This person deserves to be titled a qualified spiritual guide. His qualities in summary:

- God-fearing and pious
- Follower of Sunnah
- Has knowledge of the fundamentals of Deen.
- Acquired companionship with a pious elder to gain spirituality
- Intelligentsia and scholars are inclined towards him
- His companionship is effective
- The Seekers on the path of spirituality find their condition in his tutelage reforms and mends.

It was known in olden times the beggars would make a lion out of wool, put it on a stick and go out to beg. Meaning, the false ascetic, like the woolen lion, dons the garb of the sincere spiritual ascetic to earn worldly gains. Common people perceive Musailma, who was cunning and a liar as Ahmed (Prophet

Muhammadﷺ), who is honest, pure and genuine. Musailma bin Ḥabīb was one of a series of people (including his future wife) who claimed prophethood in 7 AD Arabia, after meeting Muhammadﷺ. He was partially deaf and blind and is considered by Muslims to be a false prophet, and is always referred to as "The Great Liar".

Eventually the dishonest face shame and humiliation, whereas the honest are victorious and assisted by Allahﷻ. Musailma earned the title of liar whereas Muhammadﷺ came to be known as the honest, wise and knowledgeable.

Muhammadﷺ is likened to the wine of Allahﷻ and pure musk, which spreads its scent as soon as its seal is broken. When Muhammadﷺ and his true followers speak, the seal of silence is broken, the world is enlightened and the soul is filled with love. Musailama's seal, and of all those who follow his way of deceit and falsehood, is filth and torment. When they speak misguidance, corruption and deception spreads.

Story III

The Bigoted King, his Vazir (minister) and the Slaying of Christians

A certain king used to persecute the Christians, desiring to exterminate their faith. His vazir persuaded him to try a strategy, namely, to mutilate the vazir himself and expel him from his court. He would then take refuge with the Christians and stir up mutual discord among them.

There is reference to such a scheme with Homer's description of Odysseus, who spied on Troy after mutilating himself.

Similarly, Zopyrus (ca. 500 BC) was a Persian nobleman mentioned in Herodotus' Histories who helped Darius I in his ascension. According to Herodotus, when Babylon revolted against the rule of Darius I, Zopyrus devised a plan to regain control of the vital city. By cutting off his own nose and ears, and then having himself whipped, he arrived at the court of Darius. Zopyrus explained that he would go before the people of Babylon and proclaim himself an exile and deserter of the Persian army punished by Darius himself. The Babylonian soldiers allowed him passage into the city and seeing a man of his high rank mutilated took his contrived story as absolute fact. Gaining the Babylonians' trust, Zopyrus soon became commander-in-chief of their army, allowing him to weaken the city's defenses. He then led soldiers under his charge into an ambush where Darius slaughtered them. The gates undefended; Darius' armies victoriously reconquered the city.[xvii]

The vazir's suggestion was adopted. He fled to the Christians and found no difficulty in persuading them that he had been treated in that barbaric way on account of his attachment to the Christian faith. He soon gained influence over them, and accepted as a saintly martyr and a divine teacher. Except for a few discerning men, all the rest were misled by him. The Christians were divided into twelve legions and each legion had a captain. To each of these captains the vazir secretly gave a volume of religious directions, taking care that each was contradictory to the other. One volume enjoined fasting as the most important religious duty, another charity, another faith, another works, and so on. After this, the vazir withdrew into a cave and refused to come out, in spite of all the entreaties of the disciples. He called the captains one by one, separately, and instructed each to set himself up as his successor after the vazir's death and use the volume given to him as a guide. He should kill anyone who opposed him, claiming this office. Then the vazir killed himself. Each captain claimed the vazir's honoured position and so the Christians were split up into many sects, each at enmity with the other. However, the malicious scheme did not succeed altogether as one faithful group remained loyal to the name of Ahmad (Muhammadﷺ) mentioned in the Gospel, and were thus saved from the destruction of the rest.[xviii]

****

Prologue

Amongst the arrogant ones was a king engaged in oppression,

An enemy of Jesus and a destroyer of Christians.

It was the epoch of Jesus and the turn was his:

He was the soul of Moses, and Moses the soul of him.

The master said to a squint-eyed, "Come on;

Go, fetch that bottle out of the room."

Said the squint-eyed one: "Which of the two bottles

Shall I bring to you? Explain fully."

"There are not two bottles," replied the master;

"Go, leave off squinting and do not be seeing more."

"O master," said he, "Don't chide me."

Said the master, "Smash one of those two."

The bottle was one, though in his eyes it seemed two;

When he broke the bottle, there was no other.

When one was broken, both vanished from sight:

A man is made squint-eyed by propensity and anger.

Anger and lust make a man squint-eyed;

They change the spirit from righteousness.

When self-interest appears, virtue becomes hidden:

A hundred veils rise from the heart to the eye.

When the judge lets bribery gain hold of his heart,

How should he know the guilty from the helpless victim?

The king, from hostility, became so squint-eyed

That, "Mercy, O Lord, mercy."

He slew hundreds of thousands of true believers, saying,

"I am the protection and support of the religion of Moses."

This story represents how a person's soul and heart become squint-eyed, meaning he can't distinguish between right and wrong when he is overcome by ego, worldly passions and lust, like the arrogant king.

A master said to his squint-eyed servant to get a bottle from the room. He went and came back, saying there were two; which one should he get. The master was very irritated and told him to leave his squint eyed-ness and look carefully. There was only one. The servant swore there were two so the master, in exasperation, told him to break one and get the other. However, when the servant broke one, there were none! In the same way, man becomes squint-eyed and myopic (wrong-sighted) through lust and anger.

Anger and lust make a man lose steadfastness, as when these two selfish motives become dominant, talent and true purpose become concealed. Firstly, a screen comes over the heart, so that its insight becomes faulty; and because the senses are often influenced by the heart, this veils the eye too. This causes error in sensual perception too. For instance, if a judge decides that he will take bribe to solve a particular case, then he can never distinguish between the victim and the oppressor. The explanation for this is that selfish motives are of two kinds; one is to gain some benefit which is desire/lust, and the other is to remove harm from oneself which is anger/rage. These are the two main reasons for injustice and inconsideration of another's gain or loss. When this is the objective, the bribing judge, for his own gain, doesn't try to investigate the truth of the matter and the real circumstances. If, by chance, he does find out the truth he will hide it from others and also try to remove it from his own conscience. In this state, the heart and conscience cannot perform to their fullest, metaphorically, a veil comes over the heart and sight. It is said that the biggest hindrance to gaining knowledge is ego, as it blocks the heart to the acceptance of the enlightenment. Humility is the first requisite to true wisdom and learning.

****

How the Christians let themselves be misguided by the vizier.

Myriads of Christian men gathered round him,

Little by little, in his abode,

He secretly expounded to them

The mysteries of Gospel and girdle and prayer.

Outwardly he was a preacher of religious commands,

But inwardly he was the whistle and snare.

On this account some Companions begged of the Prophetﷺ

The knowledge of deceitfulness of the dacoit-like soul.

Saying, "What of hidden selfish interests does it mingle

In acts of worship and in pure spiritual devotion?"

They were not seeking from him excellence of piety;

They were not inquiring where lay the outward defect.
Hair by hair, speck by speck, they were recognising
The deceitfulness of the fleshly soul as the rose from parsley.
Even the distinguished of the Companions used to
Become agitated in spirit at the warning to them.

Just like deceitful guides, the self also leads one astray. That is why the companions used to inquire from Prophet Muhammad ﷺ how the self combines hidden egotistic motives with worship and sincere intent. Huzaifa ؓ says: Everyone used to ask Prophet ﷺ about good deeds, but I used to ask him about evil so I could save myself. He did not inquire about the great rewards of obedience as much as he probed about the hidden evils of the self. All this inquiry made him an expert at recognizing the trickery and deception of the self, as easily as a man recognizes a flower from a vegetable.

From these topics of the trickery of the self, Huzaifa R.A. taught some to Hasan Basri R.A. which made his preaching and sermonizing so highly effective. Other companions, though also aware of this wisdom and knowledge, used to be astonished mainly because of his depth and insight. Some jurists and scholars claim that Huzaifa R.A. and Hasan Basri R.A. did not meet, hence by Hasan it is meant Imam Hasan R.A. However, Hasan Basri R.A. is the one most famous for his sermons and preaching, therefore, it could be that he acquired this knowledge through other companions with whom Huzaifa R.A. shared it.

****

O God, answer the crying—

What a good helper are You!

O God, there are myriads of snares and baits,

And we are like greedy, foodless birds.

From moment to moment we are caught in a fresh snare,

Though we become, each one, a falcon or a Simurgh.

Every moment You are delivering us, and again

We are going to a snare. O You who are without want!

We are putting corn in this barn,

We are losing the corn that has been garnered.

After all, do we not consider with intelligent mind

that this damage

To the corn arises from the deceitfulness of the mouse?

Since the mouse has made a hole in our barn,

And our barn has been ravaged by its guile.

O soul, in the first place prevent the mischief of the mouse,

And then show passion in garnering the corn.

Hear of the sayings related from the Chief of the Prophetsﷺ:

"No prayer is complete without 'presence'."

If there is no thievish mouse in our barn,

Where is the corn of forty years' effort?

Why is the daily sincerity not being stored,

Bit by bit, in this barn of ours?

Rumi, in a troubled frame of mind, calls out to Allahﷻ and pleads

for help in regard to the treachery of the ego and shaytan, and says, "Answer our cry for help; You are the best of Helpers." This hymn speaks about the innumerable snares and seeds (metaphor for worldly attractions that divert from the True Path) that are lying in our way. Even if we become a hawk or Simurgh (a mythical bird of great strength) we get caught in a new snare after every little while like insatiable/greedy birds. It is Your Grace that saves us from these traps every time, but then we start walking towards a new one. Meaning, deceits of the ego and shaytan are of so many kinds which ensnare in spite of sometimes being qualified and thorough in wisdom and spirituality. You grant us salvation through the guiding light of Quran and Sunnah (Prophet Muhammad's teachings), then we fall into a new deception.

Our good deeds are like a hoard of corn that keeps getting depleted. Our foolish minds cannot comprehend that a cunning mouse has made a tunnel into it and empties the stock. We do good deeds but cannot find any sign of their glow, effects and blessing. The ego and Satan create selfish motives, and diseases such as vanity, duplicity, hypocrisy, insincerity, etc. and puts to waste all our effort.

Rumi had stated that ego and Satan waste our good deeds, so now he advises to first repulse and get rid of satanic impulses like lust, selfishness, rage, etc. and the ego. Then gather your righteous deeds. Become sincere in your actions and intent; do not allow vanity and duplicity to taint them. Then your good deeds will be credible and acceptable.

To further emphasize, Rumi declares to look at the sayings of Prophet Muhammadﷺ about prayer (namaz).

Prophetﷺ said: "Remember death when you pray, for if a man remembers death when he prays, he will strive to make his prayer good. Pray the prayer of a man who does not think that he will ever pray another prayer, and beware of any matter that may require you to offer an apology."

Prayer cannot be considered complete without the presence of the heart; and presence of heart cannot be attained without getting rid of the ego and Satan. They are just like the mouse that ravages the corn gathered in the barn, without our knowing. He warns against this mouse and says that if it is not depleting our good deeds then where is the light and blessing that comes from them; why does the love of Allahﷻ and aversion of the world not manifest? If a small speck of honest and sincere deed was gathered every day, would it not become a huge pile?

Hazrat Thanvi□ says there are two ways of getting rid of bad ethics and moral values like lust, rage, etc.

One is to not have intent for them but if these feelings cross the mind and soul, to not act upon them even though there is an onslaught of these dangerous and compulsive thoughts. This status is voluntary and obligatory, whereas the onslaught of evil thoughts is involuntary and harmless.

Second way is to eradicate these immoral and harmful conducts so that there is no urge or inclination of the self for them. They would become as undesirable and despicable to nature as garbage and filth. This is desirable and a perfection of morals; it usually depends on effort, spiritual exercises and long isolations.

There are the also two ways to gain presence in prayer (salah).

First, that prayer and worship is only for the sake of Allahﷻ and not for show, or to please another for worldly gain. Without this condition prayer is not accepted and makes one deserving of punishment.

Second is to pray in such a way that there is no inclination towards any other than Allahﷻ. This again has two stages; one is that intentionally does not think of any other than Allahﷻ. This is called humility and subservience to the Only One. Second is that no other thought crosses the mind during worship except Allahﷻ.

This can only be attained by nullifying the self and all desires of the heart and mind. This is desirable but not obligatory as it is hard except for the truly pious.

Al-Quran (2:45) And seek aid in steadfast patience and prayer: and this, indeed, is a hard thing for all but the humble in spirit.

****

Many a star of fire shot forth from the iron,
And that burning heart received (it) and drew in.

But in the darkness a hidden thief

Is laying his finger upon the stars.

Extinguishing the stars one by one,

That no lamp may shine from the sky.

Though there are thousands of snares at our feet,

When You are with us there is not any trouble.

This is a parable about a thief who got into a house to steal. The master of the house tried to light a fire to see in the dark. However, before the spark could burn bright enough the thief extinguished it with his finger. The thief did this every time there was a spark. Hence, the fire could not be lighted whereby the master could save his money and belongings or be able to see the thief. In the same way, good deeds and worship are executed by the bodily organs and some luminance and blessings touch the heart, but the ego and Satan wipe it off with the help of evil conduct like rage, vanity, etc. The glow and luminescence do not collect in the heart and we cannot know because of the darkness of the soul.

Rumi addresses Allahﷻ that in spite of so many dangers on the spiritual path, there is no fear if Your attention and support is with us always. There is an indication here that the seeker should not depend on his effort and knowledge, but should plead to Allahﷻ, and look towards and depend on His grace. As Shirazi r.a. says in his verse:

Dependence on piety, knowledge and the right way is infidelity;
Even with a hundred arts you need to have faith and trust.

****

Every night You free the spirits from the body's snare,
And erase the tablets.
The spirits are set free every night from this cage,
Done with ordinance and talk and tale.
At night prisoners are unconscious of their prison,
At night governors are unconscious of their power.
There is no sorrow, no thought of gain or loss,
No fancy of this person or that person.

You, O Allahﷻ, can free us from the constraints of the evil of the ego and Satan, just as you free the soul during sleep every night from the bodily trap. The soul becomes carefree and blithe; there's no worry; It is no one's ruler and nor is it ruled. While sleeping, prisoners have no worry about the prison and kings have no care about their riches. No concern for profit or for loss, no thought of this person or that. Consequently, as You free the soul daily from such great imprisonment so that it becomes untroubled, so O Lord, make us carefree from the grief of our conscience, soul and inner turmoil.

****

This is the state of the 'arif (gnostic), even without sleep:
God said, "Consider, while they slept." Shy not at this.

He is asleep, day and night, to the affairs of the world,

like a pen in the hand of the Lord's control.

One who sees not the hand in the writing

Thinks it's the act from the pen by means of movement.

He has shown forth some part of this state of the 'arif,

The vulgar too are carried off by sleep of the senses.

Oh, in the world there is many a Man of the Cave

Beside you, before you, at this time.

The Cave is with him, the Friend is in converse with him;

But your eyes and ears are sealed, what does it avail?

Just as ordinary people are unaware and detached from their body and surroundings during sleep, so a mystic/ gnostic (arif) is in this state perpetually, without sleeping. The Quran says with regard to the people of the cave (as'haabe kahf):

Al-Quran 18:18 And thou wouldst have thought that they were awake, whereas they lay asleep……

This is only an analogy of the state of the mystic to those in the cave, who seemed to have their eyes open, but in reality were asleep. It is not meant to be the actual interpretation of the verse of the Quran. It means that the true seeker and mystic is totally oblivious to the affairs of the world. It doesn't mean he's unconscious, but that he has no inclination or attraction towards any actions or words that create a barrier between him and Allah, and no act issues forth from him that is against the pleasure of his Lord. To further clarify, the mystics are likened to a pen. They are as obedient to their Lord as a pen in the hand of the writer, who moves it where he wills. This does not mean that their actions are spontaneous or without thought because that would, first of all, be against the doctrine of the Truth, and then there would be no excellence on their part. They would be like machines and their obedience would not be established as to be from their own choice. In fact, the purpose of this example is to explain that they have annihilated their desires and choices to that of their Lord to the extent that, even though they have command over their words and deeds, they consider affairs of Shariah (laws of Islamic Jurisprudence) as part of their inherent nature over which man has no control. That is why their actions resemble those of the pen, which is dependent on the movement of the scribe; however, the movements of the pen are involuntary whereas theirs are by choice. As for actions that are involuntary and part of human disposition, for those also they look at the True Cause which is the Creator, whereas common people look at external causes. This distinguishes the mystic and gnostic from the common man with regard to knowledge and wisdom.

Just as a man who can't see the hand thinks the pen is moving on its own, similarly the common man in voluntary matters has chosen his own free will and hasn't made himself subservient to the laws of Creator. As for involuntary, innate and inherent characteristics and acts he is oblivious to the True Cause, the Creator, and thinks they are from his own choosing like a pen moving by itself.

God, in His mercy, to enlighten ordinary people about the devotion and pursuit of the arif for Truth so that they aspire for the same, imposed dreams on them while putting their worldly senses to sleep. In this way, they received some visions of the spiritual realm.

The state of unawareness of the world that ordinary people have while in their dreams is similar to the state that seekers have while awake. They have been likened to the people of the cave (ashaabe kahf, Quran:18) who seemed to be awake but were sleeping. Rumi here answers a question about where such people are that he describes. He says there are thousands of true friends of Allah around you, seemingly awake but unaware of the world, who talk to you and live with you. There is a seal on your sight and hearing due to your worldliness, so you do not recognize them or benefit from their august company.

****

Whosoever is awake is the more asleep;
His wakefulness is worse than his sleep.
When our soul is not awake to God,
Wakefulness is like closing our doors.
All day long, from the buffets of imagination
And from loss and gain and from fear of decline,
There remains to it neither joy nor grace and glory
Nor way of journeying to Heaven.

These verses reproach the worldly smartness and engrossment. The one who is worldly-wise is all the more negligent/heedless of Allahﷻ. His wakefulness is worse than his sleep where his senses are completely disabled, because in waking he gets involved in transgressions/vice/sins for worldly gains. When the focus and awareness of Allahﷻ is lost then wakefulness is like a prison.

When the soul is constantly chasing worldly goods and desires, then there is no beauty, splendour and luster to be found in it. It cannot travel towards the higher universe or perceive it because complete focus cannot be attained in two different directions.

****

The bird is flying on high, and its shadow

Is speeding on the earth, flying like a bird.

Some fool begins to chase the shadow,

Running so far that he becomes powerless,

Not knowing that it is the reflection of that bird in the air,

Not knowing where is the origin of the shadow.

He shoots arrows at the shadow;

His quiver is emptied in seeking.

The quiver of his life became empty:

His life passed in running hotly in chase of the shadow.

When the shadow of God is his nurse,

It delivers him from phantom and shadow.

The shadow of God is that servant of God

Who is dead to this world and living through God.

Lay hold of his skirt most quickly without misgiving
That you may be saved in the skirt of the last days.
He extended the shadow in the form of the saints,
Which guides to the light of the Divine Sun.

These verses explain through a parable the vain desires of the one running after the worldly life. The transitory existence of this world compared to the everlasting life of the Hereafter is like a shadow compared to a real entity. Hence the example of one who neglects the Hereafter for the sake of worldly desires is like the one who sees a bird flying in the air and its shadow reflecting on the ground. If he tries to hunt the shadow he will remain empty-handed, however fast he runs after it. He doesn't know that this shadow is only a reflection of the real bird, nor does he know where the reality of this shadow is, meaning the real bird. He keeps throwing arrows at the shadow and in this quest he empties his quiver. In the same way, the worldly seeker's quiver of life empties very quickly in search of the shadow of this transitory world.

After condemning the fantasies and desires of the world, now these verses explain how to seek salvation. That is acquired by the attentiveness and nurturing of a qualified sage (Shaikh kaamil), and compliance and obedience from the disciple. Rumi says if a "shadow of God" becomes this worldly person's guide, he can be saved from this aforementioned shadow, futile pastimes, fascination and absorption of worldly affairs. This "shadow of God" is a completely subservient slave of Allah، meaning unaware of worldly affairs like the dead and fully aware of the Truth. Hold fast onto this person without doubt so that you are saved from the trials at the time of death when faith is in danger due to excessive love of the world.

In the preceding verses shadow was resembled to the world due to its impermanence. Here the subservient slave of Allahﷻ is likened to His shadow. Just as a shadow is proof of the sun so a true slave of Allahﷻ is proof and guide towards the One True Being.

****

Though the surface of silver is white and new,
The hands and dress are blackened by it.
Although fire is red-faced with sparks,
Look at the black behaviour in its action.
If the lightning appears luminous to the eye,
From its distinctive property it is the robber of sight.

These verses refer to the unqualified and insincere spiritual guide. Outwardly his advice and solicitations seem to encourage effort towards the Truth but they do not have any mystical/spiritual effect. In fact, his words increase sloth and inertia because they lack genuineness and honesty, and are full of pretense and hypocrisy. Then to further explain the point metaphorically, Rumi says that the utterances of such fake mystics are like silver. It looks so shining and white but it blackens the hands and clothes if you rub against it. Similarly, fire is red in colour but its effect on things it burns is black; lightening is dazzling and bright, but paradoxically, damages sight.

****

The arrogant king had no scent of the unicolority of Jesus,
Nor had he a temperament from the essence of
the colour of Jesus.
From that pure colour a garment of a hundred colours
Would become as simple and one-coloured as light.
Is not unicolourity that from which weariness occurs?
No, it is like fish and clear water.
Although there are thousands of colours on dry land,
fish are at war with dryness.
Who is the fish and what is the sea in simile
That the King Almighty and Glorious should resemble them?
In existence multitude of seas and fishes prostrate themselves
In adoration before that Munificence and Bounty.

These verses refer to the story about the evil Jewish king's vizier (minister) who tries to misguide the Christians so that they forsake the religion of Isa☼ (Jesus) who was the true prophet sent to the people through Divine mercy after Moosa☼.

Rumi states that there is unity of purpose of the righteous ones (people of the True Path). They all have the same goal, the only difference is in their modus operandi (methodology). This is similar to a doctor treating two different patients who have different illnesses. He will prescribe separate medication for both but the purpose will be the same that is to balance the disposition. Accordingly, all the Prophets□ are united in their primary beliefs and teachings, but differ in their secondary for the benefit of different conditions of nations. The main purpose of each has been to gain nearness towards Allahﷻ. Hence, these verses aim to discredit the minister who regarded the religion of Moosa؏ to be contrary to Isa؏, and he did not perceive the unity of purpose of both.

The verses explain that the vizier had no understanding of the spiritual inclination of Isa؏ and his unicolority which he shared with Moosa؏. Otherwise he would have known that Isa؏ was not making people against Moosa؏. In fact he was calling people to the one same purpose which was common to both their religions, that is the concept of Unity (Tawheed). The impact of this purification was that clothes of a hundred colours, meaning people of different beliefs, become one in colour, became believers of One God in the same way as light in its true form is one-coloured, with the ability to reach Allahﷻ.

Then, to remove the doubt that this unity of the soul could cause boredom and monotony, as usually happens in worldly things that one tires of the same thing after a while Rumi uses the metaphor of fish which never tire of clear water even though there are a thousand colours and conditions on dry land. They have a severe discord and hatred for dry land. The believers of Oneness, who are figuratively termed as mahi (fish), too, can never be satiated with their attachment to the One True Being (expressed as the ocean). Boredom sets in when desire wanes, and desire wanes when magnificence and excellence diminishes or the seeker acquires the ultimate. When the gnostic's yearning never reaches its ultimate and the excellence of the One Desired never ends, there is no way of diminishing the desire. As a matter of fact, it keeps increasing. There are millions of colours and attractions in the world but the seeker is not interested because of the absorption and passion with Haq (Truth).

In the preceding verses sea has been resembled to Allahﷻ only because compared to land it has more lucidity and unity. The fish can never be satiated with the sea, just as the seeker can never have enough of the True Being due to His Oneness. The unity in the sea is external but His unity is authentic and true. Hundreds of thousands of fish and seas and everything in the universe has come into being because of Him. However, there is a correlation between the absolute unity of both and hence, the resemblance is appropriate. A similar resemblance is proven from the Quran too, where the light of Allahﷻ is compared to that of a lamp.

Al-Quran (24:35) Allah is the Light of the heavens and the earth. The Parable of His Light is as if there were a Niche and within it a Lamp: the Lamp enclosed in Glass: the glass as it were a brilliant star: Lit from a blessed Tree, an Olive, neither of the east nor of the west, whose oil is well-nigh luminous, though fire scarce touched it: Light upon Light! Allah guides whom He wills to His Light: Allah sets forth examples for men: and Allah knows all things.

****

How many a rain of generosity has rained,

So that the sea was made thereby to scatter pearls!

How many a sun of generosity has shone,

So that cloud and sea learned to be bountiful!

The sunbeams of Wisdom struck on soil and clay,

So that the earth became receptive of the seed.

The soil is faithful to its trust, and whatever you have sown in it,

You carry away the kind thereof without fraud.

It has derived this faithfulness from that faithfulness,

Inasmuch as the sun of Justice has shone upon it.

Until springtime brings the token of God,

The soil does not reveal its secrets.

The Bounteous One who gave to an inanimate thing

This information, faithfulness and righteousness,

His grace makes an inanimate thing informed;

His wrath makes blind the men of understanding.

Soul and heart cannot endure that ferment:

To whom shall I speak? There is not in the world a single ear.

Wherever there was an ear, through Him it became an eye;

Wherever there was a stone, through Him it became a jasper.

He is an alchemist - what is alchemy?

He is a giver of miracles - what is magic?

These verses establish and reinforce the concept of the previous verses that all creation is dependent on the Creator. Hence, the sparkle of the ocean is due to the blessings and benevolence of

Allahﷻ that have showered on it. The generosity of rain and oceans which grant so much water, pearls and a million other bounties to the world is the special endowment from Allah'sﷻ attribute of beneficence. The sun's property of spreading light is the munificence emanating from the Creator. The soil accepts the seed and cultivates it into plants. For this it needed knowledge which was granted by the Creator from His own attribute of cognition. Then there is the quality of trust and integrity in the soil; as you sow, so shall you reap. It does not happen that it will bring forth barley from the seeds of wheat. It has acquired the quality of trustworthiness for which integrity is required, from its Benefactor, the One True Being, because He is Trustworthy (Ameen), even though Ameen is not in the famous names of Allahﷻ.

Moreover, the sign that soil is knowledgeable and aware is from the fact that it doesn't bring forth its bounty and does not take out its plants and flowers until spring brings the command of its Creator. It is from the overflowing benevolence of Allahﷻ that an inanimate object, soil, becomes like an animate object with endowments of knowledge and action. The manifestation of His aesthetic attributes grant even inanimate objects insight and intelligence, whereas His majestic and august attributes make the most knowledgeable and intelligent, which is Man, like the blind. They cannot see the Truth like Iblis (Satan) and Bal'am, a pious scholar from the children of Israel who strayed from his true path, followed his vain desires and invited the wrath of

Allah﷾. He is likened to a dog in the Quran, which is a far lesser being than Man, which is the ultimate degradation of the lofty station granted to him.

Al-Quran (7:176) If it had been Our will, We should have elevated him with Our signs; but he inclined to the earth, and followed his own vain desires. His similitude is that of a dog: if you attack him, he lolls out his tongue, or if you leave him alone, he (still) lolls out his tongue. That is the similitude of those who reject Our signs; So relate the story; perchance they may reflect.

It is important to understand that the Divine attributes are beyond the grasp of man. Allah﷾ is Unique in them and not all attributes are manifest in the creation. Also, repugnant, negative and obnoxious traits found in man are only because of corruption and depravity on his own part.

Rumi further discloses more mysteries of the Divine Greatness and Power. He declares his heart and soul do not have the strength to curb his passions. He wants to say more but there is none who has the capacity to listen. Most people either refuse to listen as they do not understand or are afflicted by disbelief and atheism.

Then he goes on to praise the quality of listening with acceptance, because that develops into a vision through Divine grace. Certitude of knowledge is converted into certitude of perception; just as a mere stone converts into jasper with healing properties beneficial for strength and stability. **Hence with acceptance and supplication the deficient becomes perfect.**

In praise of the Almighty, he says the powers of an alchemist are nothing compared to Him. The main goal of alchemists was to turn base metal into gold and to attain the Philosopher's stone, a substance that would bring perfection to life. Allahﷻ is the True Alchemist as He Alone has the power to turn a deficient human being into a spiritually perfect soul; He Alone is the True Giver of miracles.

****

The vizier was ignorant and heedless, like the king:
He was wrestling with the eternal and inevitable.
With a God so Mighty that in a moment He causes a hundred
Worlds like ours to come into existence from non-existence.
A hundred worlds like ours He displays to the sight,
When He makes your eye seeing by Himself.
If the world appears to you vast and bottomless,
Know that to Omnipotence it is but an atom.
This world, indeed, is the prison of your souls:
Oh, go in yonder direction, for there lays your open country.
This world is finite, and truly that is infinite:
Image and form are a barrier to that Reality.
The multitudes of Pharaoh's spears
Were shattered by Moses with a single staff.
Multitude were the therapeutic arts of Galen:
Before Jesus and his breath they were a laughing-stock.
Multitude were the books of poems:
At the word of an Illiterateﷺ they were shame.

Rumi comes back to the story of the Jewish king and his vizier, who try to misguide the Christians so that they forsake the religion of Isa who was the true prophet sent to the people after Moosa through Divine mercy.

Like the king, the vizier was also ignorant and oblivious to the extent that he was trying to defy the Eternal Lord of the universe, Creator of each and every being. The vizier's defiance was to try and eradicate Christianity when Allah had decreed that it would be the prevalent and recognized religion of that era. He is Alive, all power belongs to Him, He was, is and always will be, He is unique in His excellence. How could the vizier dare to confront the One whose might was such that He could create a thousand more such universes as this from nothingness in the blink of an eye? He can grant insight to any He chooses, meaning true cognizance of His being. Then the heart and soul have a vision far beyond this world which seems dark and confined compared to the wide expanse of the spiritual world.

Rumi talks about the unworthiness of this world in the face of the Almighty. This world seems vast and limitless to you but it is like a speck compared to the might of the Creator which is incomparable and limitless. In fact, as much as you are engrossed in this world it is the prison of your souls.

Messenger of Allah said: The world is a prison for the believer and Paradise for the disbeliever.

Be mindful of the spiritual world as that is immense, this world is limited and that world limitless. Rumi compares the weakness and strength of both this world and the spiritual world. Thousands of staffs of the pharaoh's magicians were defeated by just one staff of Moosa﷽. The magicians' staffs were the product of this world whereas Moosa's﷽ staff was from the Other World.

Similarly, Galen was a Greek physician in the Roman Empire. Greeks followed his teachings and were considered experts in medical sciences, yet in front of one life-giving breath of Isa﷽ their skills were an object of ridicule. Isa﷽ was endowed with the strength of the spiritual world whereas the Greek physicians' skills were from the mortal world.

The Quraish of Makkah in the time of Prophet Muhammadﷺ were considered the most eloquent. Their poems could fill thousands of books, yet compared to the eloquence of the Noble Quran through the tongue of the unlettered Prophet Muhammadﷺ they were a disgrace. The oration of the Quraish was acquired from this world whereas the word of Allah﷽ through which Muhammadﷺ spoke was a miracle from the world beyond.

****

With such an all-conquering Lord,
How should anyone not die, unless he be a vile wretch?
Many a mind as a mountain did He uproot;
The cunning bird He hung up by its two feet.
To sharpen the intelligence and wits is not the way:
None but the broken wins the favour of the King.

This discourse is on the supremacy and complete dominance of Allahﷻ. In front of such Absolute Power who would not die, meaning assume humility and defeat, unless he was damned and shameful. His power is such that many who were like mountains in their determination and steadfastness were uprooted from their status and position of glory, for example Bal'am and Barseesa.

Bal'am bin Baura was a scholar of great standing and status. He had been granted the knowledge of the wonderful and most powerful great name of Allahﷻ that causes any supplication to be instantly accepted. However, blinded by the love of his wife and wealth, he tried to harm Moosa۔ but did not succeed. The punishment that was meted out to Bal'am has been recorded in the Quran.

Al-Quran (7:176) "Thus his (Bal'am) likeness is as the likeness of a dog."

Barṣīṣā, was a saintly recluse whose worship and devotion to Allahﷻ was so great that he was called the great worshipper from the Children of Israel. He was given care of a sick woman by her three brothers, who were going on a journey. At the devil's suggestion Barṣīṣā seduced the woman. When he discovered that she has conceived, Barṣīṣā killed her and the child, and buried their bodies to hide evidence of his sin. The devil, however, revealed the murder to the woman's brothers. The devil said to Barṣīṣā he will save him on the condition that he prostrates before him as a sign of the devil's greatness. Panic-stricken, he again succumbed to the devil, renouncing God in return for safety, only to be mocked by Satan.

Al-Quran (59:15-17) [Theirs is] like the example of those shortly before them: they tasted the bad consequence of their affair, and they will have a painful punishment. [Satan said]: "I am free of you; I fear Allah, the Lord of the Worlds." So the outcome for both of them is that they will be in the Fire, abiding eternally therein. And that is the recompense of the wrong-doers.

The metaphor of the bird is given to show how cleverness and intelligence is not the way to the Lord. When a hunter wants to capture a parrot he passes a string through a hollow reed and ties both ends to the branch of a tree. When the parrot sits on it, it spins so the parrot, in fear, holds it tight with both claws and gets trapped. This enables the hunter to catch the parrot. The intellectuals, just like the parrot, deduce through corrupt, vain logic and are thus deceived through misguidance and ignorance. Subjugation and humility is the only way to the Lord.

Muhammad said: Allah says, "I am with those whose hearts are broken for My sake."

Imam Munawi mentions this narration when explaining the words of the Prophet, "The most afflicted of people in this world is a Messenger or a righteous servant." **Through affliction,**

the desires melt away and hearts are lowered in front of Allahﷻ allowing one's rank to increase in His eyes.

Imam Qurtubi said, "Allah loves to afflict his chosen servants in order to perfect their virtues and to raise their rank with Him. This is neither a flaw for them nor a punishment."

Ibn `Ajibah cites it in the context of explaining the broken-heartedness of the sinner, stating that the performance of good works that leads to arrogance and pride is worse than the performance of something sinful that results in sincere regret. Rather, this state of regret, lowliness, and debasement is in fact the reality of true servitude.

However, this does not mean that knowledge and effort are useless. It is just a message of caution to not succumb to arrogance after acquiring knowledge and putting in effort because no plans or strategies are effective in the face of the dominance and power of the Almighty. **Understand that gaining knowledge and putting in effort is obligatory but keep the focus on the grace and mercy of the Lord.**

This verse says it well:

Depending on virtue and knowledge and principles is falseness;
Even if you have a hundred skills you must have
faith to reach your destination.

****

> **Your spirit was bearing you towards the highest sphere:**
> **You went towards the water and the clay amongst the lowest.**
> **By this fall you metamorphosed yourself from that existence**
> **Which was the envy of the intelligences.**
> **Consider, then, how is this metamorphosis compared**
> **With that metamorphosis. This is exceedingly disgraceful.**
> **After all, you are a son of Adam. O degenerate!**
> **How long will you regard lowness as nobility?**
> **How long will you say, "I will conquer a whole world,**
> **I will make this world full of myself"?**
> **If the world should be filled with snow from end to end,**
> **The glow of the sun would melt it with a single look.**
> **You urged the steed of ambition towards the stars:**
> **You did not acknowledge Adam who was worshipped.**

Your soul aspires to rise to spiritual loftiness and for nearness to Allahﷻ through His remembrance but your focus is on clay and water, that is, dominance of the lowly desires of the self. You fell into the abyss that distanced you from Allahﷻ and banished from you an existence which was predominantly based on spiritual love and discernment. It was the envy of the angels. The person whose natural disposition is dictated by spiritual ethics, love, knowledge, obedience and remembrance of Allahﷻ rather than lust, rage, negligence and sins, is superior to certain angels. This is because angels have no impulse or impetus for wrongdoing, so the absence of sins is not strange. In man, because of an inborn, natural inclination for transgression and recklessness, the absence of sin is strange. It is an evidence of his struggle to reach for his true worth and introspection within his soul.

Al-Quran (4:28) And man is created weak.

Al-Quran (33:72) Surely he is very unjust, very ignorant.

Human beings suffer from ignorance and injustice. The unjust act is not restricted to others. It can be applied to the person himself by acting against his own good for the gratification of his ego.

At the same time, man has been endowed control to direct his temperament to any direction he wants. He can even use it to acquire infinite perfection.

Al-Quran (103:2-3) Most surely man is in loss, except for those who have believed and done righteous deeds and advised each other to truth and advised each other to patience.

Often, vices are caused by man himself, by his free will and are not due to nature. For example, if a he is a liar, this is because he himself has chosen that. The inherent vices in man cannot prevent him from attaining perfection. Man has been gifted the highest form of intelligence, capabilities and potentials as well as freewill.

Al-Quran (65:1) Every person who breaks Divine laws, has oppressed himself.

If a person does not pray or fast then he has been unjust to himself. When a person does not fulfill his duties to family, society or the world at large, robs, corrupts or harms others in any way he is initially doing a disservice to himself than to others.

The consequences of his ill acts will destroy his inherent God-given superiority. He initiates hindrances on the way to his perfection.

Rumi says all your effort and exertion is for the gain of the desires of the flesh. In all this you failed to know Adam⬚, who was the object of prostration by the angels. O forsaken one, you were his son; then why did you destroy your value and glory for worldly gains? How long will you continue to think of baseness and lowliness as dignity and progress? How long will you pursue desires for the gratification of your egoistic self?

Al-Quran (17:11) And man prays for evil as he ought to pray for good and man is ever hasty.

Selfish desires are like the snow; the sun of Destiny and the decree of the One True Being will annihilate them and there will be no trace left of your grand achievements. Life becomes immortal when spent for the greater purpose of self and others through compassion, love and service.

****

God by a single spark makes useless his burden
And of a hundred Viziers and a hundred thousand.
He makes the essence of that imagination to be wisdom;
He makes the essence of that poisoned water to be a drink.
That which raises doubt He turns into certainty;
He makes loving kindnesses grow from the causes of hatred.
He cherishes Abraham in the fire;
He turns fear into security of spirit.

You worry about your mortal relationships but their comparison to the True Love of Allah﷾ is like that of a load of firewood to a mere spark. In as much as the love of that person, or even thousands of such persons weigh heavily on your heart, one spark of the True Divine love can shatter and destroy it. Verily, such is the effect of True Love that worldly relationships of a lifetime are wiped out so that no trace is left.

Foolish fantasies are converted into pure wisdom and beneficial knowledge through His implementation.

There are many ways evil fantasies and destructive knowledge can be changed to beneficial wisdom.

1. A person becomes well aware of evil and misguidance through experience; hence is not deceived by anyone.

    I got to know evil not from evil, but to watch out for it;

    For the one who does not know evil from goodness falls into it.

2. A person has the strength of inference and the power of reasoning, previously used for corrupt desires and worthless purposes. Now he uses these strengths for sincere purposes and to gain True Knowledge. This will guide others and grant them insight too.

    Messenger of Allahﷺ said: People are like gold and silver; those who were best in Jahiliyyah (Pre-Islamic Period of Ignorance) are best in Islam.

Messenger of Allah said: For whomever Allah wants good, he gives him understanding to the Right Way.

3. A person uses his awareness and experience to compare True knowledge with worthless knowledge. This increases the value of beneficial knowledge in his eyes.

4. He can respond appropriately to this meaningless knowledge with the use of his intelligence.

5. He has had his fill from these worldly pursuits and schemes, and faced their negative consequences. He has no more yearnings and inclinations for them, as when a person matures or reaches old age.

6. He can satisfy his own soul, as well as others', by analyzing religious narrations to intellectual matters. For example, just as certain matters of lawmaking are beyond the understanding of common man, similarly, if the mysteries of Divine Decree cannot be understood it is ignorance to refute them.

These above points explain how Divine Decree can convert undesirable knowledge to advantageous and favourable knowledge.

Next Rumi talks about undesirable morals and ethics and how they destroy the soul of self and others. However, the power of the Almighty is such that He can change poison into nectar and bad morals into praiseworthy ones for the seeker through man's effort and passion.

The same evil morals which caused distance from Allah﷾ and enmity among people become a source of nearness to Allah and loving kindness to others.

This basically means that the inherent characteristic of a person does not change; his use of them changes.

For example, a person is miserly and hot-tempered. When he is refined through effort and desire for the nearness of Allah﷾, his anger is now directed towards his egoistic self rather than others. His miserliness, which previously prevented generosity in spending for good causes, is now directed at stopping those extravagant spending that are against the pleasure of Allah﷾.

This confirms that inherent nature of things cannot be changed but the command is for effort and practice to change the use of the given characteristics for greater good.

 The Messenger of Allahﷺ exclaimed: If you hear that a mountain has moved from its place, believe it; but if you hear that a man's nature has changed, don't believe it, for he remains true to his inborn disposition.

Coming back to the might of the All Powerful, Rumi gives the example of how the fire in which infidels threw Ibrahimﷺ changed from a source of fear into a source of peace and calm. If He can do this, then He can as easily convert evil morals into noble characteristics.

****

Put cotton-wool in the ear of the low sense;

Take off the bandage of sense from your eyes!

The ear of the head is the cotton-wool of the ear of the

conscience:

Until the former becomes deaf, that inward is deaf.

Become without sense and without ear and without thought,

That you may hear the call, 'Return!'"

So long as you are in the conversation of wakefulness,

How will you catch any scent of the conversation of sleep?

Our speech and action is the exterior journey:

The interior journey is above the sky.

The sense saw dryness, because it was born of dryness:

The Jesus of the spirit set foot on the sea.

The journey of the dry body happened on dry land,

The journey of the spirit took place in the heart of the sea.

Shut down your physical senses so that your mystical senses (deeper insight) can flow. Refine your soul so you gain spiritual abundance, which is the real existence, rather than just living in the worldly sphere.

Your physical senses are a prison for your spiritual insight. Until such time as physical hearing is not deaf, spiritual hearing will remain deaf.

The soul cannot focus on two different directions at the same time.

As long as you will remain engrossed in worldly passions through these physical senses, perceptions of the inner self, your spiritual state and the discipline of your soul are impossible to achieve. Hence, if you want spiritual perception and insight, empty yourself of all physical senses and intellectual prowess. Use your innate intelligence to achieve spiritual perfection. Then you will become the tranquil soul worthy of the address "Irjayi" (Return) on the Day of Judgement.

Al-Quran (89:27-28) [But to the righteous Allah will say,] "O you human being that has attained to inner peace! Return to your Sustainer, well-pleased [and] pleasing [Him].

When the physical senses become subdued, the soul acquires tranquility and becomes qualified to hear this address.

Rumi explains this through a simile. If you are busy in worldly discussion it's not possible to be in a state of dreaming. Consider the physical world as a state of wakefulness and the spiritual world as a state of dreaminess. Focus on the one will make it impossible to focus on the other.

These are clear instructions that attainment of inner light is dependent on solitude and meditation. These are dependent on being oblivious to worldly affairs in spite of conducting the daily affairs, and this, in turn, is dependent on lessening worldly ties and relationships while maintaining the rights and duties. The soul is like a ship and the world and all its obligations like the water. As long as the ship is clear of water it will sail, but when water enters the ship and overpowers it, it will drown. When worldly bonds are less, there is less worry, when there is lesser worry there is greater focus on the Other World, which will help attain knowledge and conditions of spirituality and insight.

The physical senses have been compared to dryness, as in solids, because they are made of matter, whereas spirituality has been compared to water. The soul is like Isa﷽ and Moosa﷽ in being able to cross the river of faith.

- Once someone asked Isa﷽,"How are you able to walk on water?" He replied, "With certainty." Then someone said, "But we also have certainty!" Isa﷽ then asked them, "Are stone, clay, and gold equal in your eyes?" They replied, "Certainly not!" Isa﷽ responded, "They are in mine."

- Isa﷽, the son of Maryam﷽, was known to have said, "Love of this world is the source of every wrong action, and there is much harm in wealth." They asked, "What is its harm?"
  Isa﷽ replied, "Its possessor is never safe from pride and arrogance." They said, "What if he is free of those two? Is there still harm?" Isa﷽ responded, "Yes, for by nurturing his wealth, he is diverted from the remembrance of God."

- Prophet Isa﷽ was asked "O Isa! How do you walk on the water?" He replied: "With my faith in Allah﷽." They said: "But we also have faith as you have faith, and we also believe as you believe." Isa﷽ said: "So come and walk." So they walked with him on the waves, and then drowned. Isa said to them: "What happened to you?" They said: "We are frightened of the waves." Isa replied: "Do you not fear the Lord of the waves?"

Then he took them out of the water. Then he stroked the earth with his hands, and took its dust, and when he opened them, there was gold in one hand and pebbles in another. He asked them: "Which do you like most?" They said: "Gold." He said "But they are just the same to me."

- **Al-Quran (26:63-68)** Then We revealed to Moosa: 'Strike the sea with your stick.' And it parted, and each separate part (of that sea water) became like a huge mountain. Then We brought near the others (Pharaoh's people) to that place. And We saved Moosa and all those with him. Then We drowned the others. Verily, in this is indeed a sign (or a proof), yet most of them are not believers. And verily, your Lord, He is truly, the All-Mighty, the Most Merciful.

More reasons for comparing the spiritual existence to water and physical being to solids:

1. Water is the substance of life, as opposed to matter.

   Al-Quran (21:30) and [that] We made out of water every living thing (only relevant section quoted)

   In the same way, spirituality is the source of life for the soul whereas worldliness causes negligence towards Allah which is death of the soul though the body is living.

2. Water, like spirituality, has expanse as opposed to solids. It does not stop flowing despite barriers, like the soul, whereas mortal world is like solids, limited, tangible and defined.

3. There is clarity and lucidity in the river, whereas land has composition and structure.

Spirituality desires unity but in the mortal universe excess is desirable. That is why symbolically scholars have interpreted land and sea in the following verse of Quran as the physical world and the metaphysical world respectively.

Al-Quran (17:70) Now indeed, We have conferred dignity on the children of Adam, and borne them over land and sea…. (only relevant portion of verse quoted)

****

Since your life has passed in travelling on land,
Now mountain, now river, now desert,
From where will you gain the Water of Life?
Where will you part the waves of the Sea?
The waves of earth are our imagination
And understanding and thought;
The waves of water are self-effacement
And intoxication and death (annihilation).
While you are in this intoxication,
You are far from that intoxication.
While you are drunk with this,
You are blind to that cup.

Outward speech and talk is as dust:
For a time make a habit of silence. Take heed!

O you, whose life so far has been deprived of spirituality, do not think that your soul does not have the capacity for it. In fact, you have spent your whole life in worldly affairs and ties of kinship, likening it to journeying through the mountains, deserts and lands, wandering here and there. When you have spent your whole life in pursuing worldly desires how can you expect to be granted the fountain of life, which is spiritual awareness.

As long as you're drunk with the love of this world you will be distant from the sweetness of spirituality. Since talking is part of worldly ties that too focuses the heart towards the material world. This talking is like dust that covers the heart and blocks it from the light of spirituality. Hence, assume silence and keep your consciousness and focus on your heart and soul, reduce speech and meditate.

****

Lay on the beast a burden in proportion to its endurance,
Lay on the weak a task in proportion to their strength.
The bait for every bird is according to its measure;
How should a fig be the food for every bird?
If you give a babe bread instead of milk,
Take it that the poor babe will die of the bread.
Afterwards, when it grows teeth,

That babe will of its own accord ask for bread.
When an immature bird begins to fly,
It becomes a mouthful for any greedy cat.
When it grows wings, it will fly of itself without trouble
And without whistling, good or bad.

These metaphors are meant for the spiritual guide/teacher/mentor. They should not teach or deal with the disciple/pupil/protégé beyond their capacity because they will be destroyed as in the example of beast, bird and babe. Similarly, succession of power should not be handed over to the undeserving/unmerited as in the example of a newborn bird which cannot fly. If a beginner is treated like an expert and handed responsibility beyond his competence, he will create havoc and destroy his own self too. He is in need of righteous mentoring until he attains necessary skill and prowess, otherwise due to inexperience he could get afflicted with misguidance and deception.

****

Before the painter and the brush the picture is helpless
And bound like a child in the womb.
Before Omnipotence all the people of the court of audience
Are as helpless as the fabric before the needle.
Now He makes the picture the Devil, now Adam;
Now He makes the picture of joy, now of grief.

There is no power that he should move a hand in defense;
No speech, that he should utter a word concerning
injury or benefit.
Recite from the Quran the interpretation of the verse:
God said, You did not throw when you threw.
If we let an arrow fly, that is not from us: we are the bow,
And the shooter of the arrow is God.

A man is helpless regarding the decree of the Almighty, just as the picture under the brush, a child in the mother's womb and the embroidered fabric under the needle. The Creator defines the evil and good, joy and sorrow for the creation. It has no power or strength to change the work of the One True Being, nor words to complain or react from its benefit or harm.

Find confirmation of the above verses from the Quran, regarding the battle of Badr in 624 AD, which ended with a complete victory for the Muslims.

Al-Quran (8:17) You killed them not, but Allah killed them. And you (Muhammadﷺ) threw not when you did throw (a handful of dust) but Allah threw, that He might test the believers by a fair trial from Him. Verily, Allah is All-Hearing, All-Knowing.

Hence, if we shoot an arrow, then we are only the bow which is in the hands of the Shooter, Allahﷻ, who is the True Executor.

Though the Quran only mentions a particular incident, the throwing of dust, it is similar to all possible acts and established as a general rule from the indication of the Quranic text.

In these verses Rumi declares Allahﷻ as the Doer and the slave as the tool, but in a certain context the rule could reverse. Metaphorically, Allahﷻ becomes the Tool and the slave becomes the doer. This happens when the slave, through effort, discipline and pursuit becomes such that all his evil attributes and causes of lust, anger, etc. become non-existent. Noble deeds and pious acts issue forth from him effortlessly, whereas obnoxious and vile acts become almost non-existent.

Prophet Muhammadﷺ said: Allahﷻ says, "My slave approaches Me with nothing more beloved to Me than what I have made obligatory upon him, and My slave keeps drawing nearer to Me with voluntary works until I love him. And when I love him, I am his hearing with which he hears, his sight with which he sees, his hand with which he seizes, and his foot with which he walks. If he asks me, I will surely give to him, and if he seeks refuge in Me, I will surely protect him".

This status is achieved when the slave maximizes and intensifies his supererogatory acts like voluntary prayer, fasting, meditation and diminishes selfish desires.

✳✳✳✳✳✳✳✳✳

This is not jabr (compulsion);
It is the meaning of jabbari (almightiness).
The mention of Almightiness
Is for the sake of humility.

Our humility is evidence of necessity;

Our sense of guilt is evidence of freewill.

If there were not freewill, what is this shame?

And what are sorrow, guilty confusion and confusion?

Why is there scolding between masters and pupils?

Why is the mind changing from plans?

And if you say that he takes no heed of His compulsion,

God's moon has become hidden in His cloud,

There is a good answer to this. If you listen,

You will relinquish unbelief and incline towards the religion.

Remorse and humility occur at the time of illness:

The time of illness is wholly wakefulness.

At the time when you are becoming ill,

You pray God to forgive your trespass.

The foulness of your sin is shown to you;

You resolve to come back to the Way.

You make promises and vows that henceforth

Your chosen course will be nothing but obedience.

Therefore it has become certain

That illness gives to you conscience and wakefulness.

Note, then, this principle, O you that seek the principle;

Everyone who suffers pain has caught the scent.

The more wakeful any one is the fuller of suffering he is;

The more aware he is, the paler he is in countenance.

The previous verses state that all control is with the Almighty and through this some lesser intelligent people might think that religion is all dominance and force. These verses negate this belief. The control is only to establish the Almightiness of Allahﷻ as our free will is subordinate to His will. We have choice, and religion is a condition between dominance and free will. When a shameful act is issued from us we feel guilty and that is proof that it was through our free will. Similarly, the example of the teacher rebuking the pupil and encouraging effort is evidence of free will. All these stand to reason that we see the effects of free will in our daily affairs all the time.

These verses are a discourse on the previous verses which established that religion is a condition between authority and free will. Some may doubt that a person feels remorse at his vile acts not because of his free will, but unawareness of a matter that is as clear as the moon. He thinks he is responsible for his corrupt behavior because he has no knowledge of the control of the Almighty in all his affairs. It is hidden from him due to the clouds of his ignorance. Rumi states to such a skeptic there is an excellent answer if you listen carefully, stay away from disbelief and cynicism, and are inclined to the True Faith.

The regret and repentance that you feel at the time of illness is caused due to complete wakefulness and awareness. When you are ill you ask forgiveness and expiate for all your sins. The ugliness of sins becomes evident to you. You begin to make promises that now nothing will be acceptable to you except obedience to the Only One. Hence, two conditions are proven and established:

1. Illness removes ignorance and negligence to the extent that he can see the consequences of immoral actions and words.

2. He repents in illness. Now, according to the skeptic, this repentance on wicked actions was due to his ignorance that Allah﷾ had complete authority in all his affairs. However, that ignorance was removed at the time of illness; he could see his actions and their effects clearly. Then why is he ashamed of his sinful ways and why is he seeking forgiveness?

Hence, in spite of the ending of ignorance, this repentance and shame is clear proof that definitely man has choice and the power of intent in his affairs to a certain extent.

The previous verses stated bodily pain and illness as a source of awareness and knowing. In relation to this, Rumi begins to explain the magnificence of heartache.

Understand the general rule that the one who has the pain of love will find the way to the beloved.

The one who is more awakened with love will be more fulfilled; and the one more aware will have the manner of a true lover. Love joins the lover to the beloved.

Prophetﷺ narrated that Allah﷾, says, "If the servant draws near to Me a hand span, I draw near to him an arm's length; and if he draws near to Me an arm's length, I draw near to him a fathom's length. And if he comes to Me walking, I come to him running".

Muhammadﷺ said: A person will be with whom he loves.

****

If you are aware of His jabr (compulsion),

where is your humility?

Where is your feeling of the chain of

His jabbari (Almightiness)?

How one should make merry who is bound in chains?

When does the captive in prison behave like the man who is

free?

And if you consider that your foot is shackled

The king's officers are sitting over you,

Then do not act like an officer towards the helpless,

Inasmuch as that is not the nature and habit of a helpless man.

Since you do not feel His compulsion, do not say;

And if you feel it, where is the sign of your feeling?

In every act for which you have inclination,

You are clearly conscious of your power.

In every act for which you have no inclination

and desire, in regard to that

You have become a fatalist, saying, "This is from God."

These verses continue with the discourse for those who believe that man is helpless and has no control over his affairs. Allah is the Supreme Authority. If that is the case, then how is it that your weakness and powerlessness cannot be seen? You defy the commands of your Lord and do not refrain from imposing your will. In fact, you exert power over others and oppress the weak.

This means that your heart does not accept the doctrine of predestination and man's helplessness over his affairs. Why then do you make this false claim and make objections to the concept of free will?

How does a man in chains, as you claim with your belief of predestination, enjoy life? How does a captive act as freely as you do, with complete disregard of the Divine command? The result is that this whole argument has two aspects; either you believe in predestination or don't. If you don't believe then don't make verbal claims. If you believe, then show the signs of feebleness, submission and oppression.

These verses define the confusion of the egoistic self, as predestination is just an excuse. In reality the main purpose is to attain selfish desires. In acquiring things that you desire, you use your power and capability and strive towards them. For things that you have no desire for, you make yourself helpless, that this is from the Almighty. If you really believe in predestination, then why do you use your resources and power to gain things you desire? This shows that your belief in the doctrine of predestination is just an excuse to gratify your ego.

✳✳✳✳✳✳✳✳✳

The Prophets are fatalistic in regard to the works of this world,
The unbelievers are fatalistic in regard to the works
of the next world.
To the Prophets the works of the next world are freewill;

To the foolish the works of this world are freewill.

Because every bird flies to its own kind:

It behind, and its life and desire before it.

Inasmuch as the unbelievers were related to Sijjin (Hell),

They were agreeable to the prison (sijn) of this world.

Inasmuch as the Prophets were related to 'Illiyyin (Heaven),

They went towards the 'Illiyyin of spirit and heart.

Inasmuch as God comes not into sight,

These prophets are the vicars of God.

Nay, I have said wrongly; for if you suppose that the vicar

And He who is represented by the vicar are two,

it is bad, not good.

Nay; they are two so long as you are a worshipper of form,

They have become one to him who has escaped from form.

People sometimes become powerless in their affairs and sometimes become passionate and forceful in the attainment of their desires. This means they accept both aspects, predestination and free will, and, in fact, existence of both is the real truth. Then Rumi goes on to give advice as to when helplessness should be predominant so that one should be resigned to fate, and when to prefer effort for attaining the desired outcome. Explaining through examples, Rumi says Prophets□ were fatalistic in affairs of the world but exerted effort to acquire the resources of the Hereafter. Disbelievers are fatalistic in affairs of the Hereafter, but strive in attainment of worldly desires. This is because every bird flies to its own species; meaning the disbelievers are from those of the Hell-fire, hence they seek worldly desires, whereas the Prophets are befitting for the Heavenly abode and so they focused their heart and soul on it. They were passionate to struggle for the Hereafter.

Obligatory and real existence is only for Allah. If actual existence is considered, then all things created by Allah are present in form, they have substance, are measurable and changeable. However, if one transcends form and physical being, then the Creator and the created are one.

****

When you look at the form, your eye is two;
Look at its light, which grew from the eye.
It is impossible to distinguish the light of the two eyes,
When a man has cast his look upon their light.
If ten lamps are present in place,
Each differs in form from another.
To distinguish without any doubt the light of each,
When you turn your face towards their light, is impossible.
If you count a hundred apples or a hundred quinces,
They do not remain a hundred, become one,
when you crush them.
In things spiritual there is no division and no numbers;
In things spiritual - there is no partition and no individuals.

All these are examples to explain the concept of how there can be unity in two things, and yet, at the same time diversity. Just as all prophets are different and yet, they are one in the spirit of prophethood, meaning we cannot differentiate between them in their light of guidance. We can also not deny one and validate another. For a true believer all prophets mentioned in the book of Allah﷾ are to be believed.

Al-Quran (2:285) They all believe in God, and His angels, and His revelations, and His apostles, making no distinction between any of His apostles; (only relevant portion of verse quoted)

The creation, in form and space, is in numbers, but the only True Being is One, the Creator, Everlasting and Eternal.

****

Sweet is the oneness of the Friend with His friends:
Hold onto the foot of spirit because form is headstrong.
Make headstrong form waste away with tribulation,
That beneath it you may see Unity, like a treasure.
And if you waste it not away, His favours will waste it —
Oh, my heart is His disciple.
He even shows Himself to hearts,
He sews the tattered frock of the dervish.

Rumi says become so engrossed with the True Being that your focus moves away from materialistic resources, because that is the desired state of eternal love. By tribulation he means effort and passion for Allah﷾. The material world is headstrong and disobedient, so through this engrossment with Allah, waste it away so it fades into inexistence. Then Rumi says to the one on this path of spirituality that even if your effort and striving can't wipe it out, then His mercy will wipe out all the attractions of the material world. My heart is His slave when I perceive His attention and vigilance.

You walk on His path and He will provide the fruit of your labour.

The knowledge and understanding of Allahﷻ is not acquired but gifted after effort is made to please Him. Just as the end result of drinking water to quench thirst, taking medication to treat illness or, reflection to come to the right decision, etc., all of these are dependent on Allah'sﷻ will.

However, as a rule, Allah grants when effort is made, because the world is based on cause and effect.

He usually does not give without endeavor. Hence, man should strive, exert and desire, but at the same time realize that achievement of purpose is only through Allah's mercy.

****

Simple were we and all one substance;
We were all without head and without foot yonder.
We were one substance, like the Sun;
We were knotless and pure, like water.
When that goodly Light took form,
It became number like the shadows of a battlement.
Raze the battlement with the catapult (manjaniq)

That difference may vanish from amidst this company.

I would have explained this with contention,

But I fear lest some mind may stumble.

The points are sharp as a sword of steel;

If you have not the shield, turn back and flee!

Do not come without shield against this adamant,

For the sword is not ashamed of cutting.

For this cause I have put the sword in sheath,

That none who misreads may read contrariwise.

We come to complete the tale

And of the loyalty of the multitude of the righteous,

Who rose up after this leader (the corrupt vazir),

Demanding a vicar in his place.

One of those leaders advanced

And went before that loyal-minded people.

"Behold," said he," I am that man's vicar:

I am the vicar of Jesus at the present time.

Look, this scroll is my proof

That after him the caliphate belongs to me."

Another amir came forth from ambush:

His claim regarding the caliphate was the same.

He too produced a scroll from under his arm,

So that in both there arose the Jewish anger.

The rest of the amirs, one after another,

Drawing swords of keen mettle,

Each with a sword and a scroll in his hand

Fell to combat like raging elephants.

Hundreds of thousands of Christians were slain,

So that there were mounds of severed heads.
Blood flowed, on left and right, like a torrent;
Mountains of this dust rose in the air.
The seeds of dissension which the vazir had sown
Had become a calamity to their heads.

In the previous verses Rumi talked about the seeker gaining knowledge of the One True Being and how to acquire it. There has to be accord between the lover and the Beloved, and so he talks about the spiritual world where we were in a simple form and in single core. There was no composition, structure or plurality. In that existence we had no body or limbs; we were devoid of form like the sun. We were fluid like water. When this pure light of the spirit was attached to the body it became numerous and multiple. That one spirit became many as it attached to different bodies just like the rays of the sun falling on a rampart of a castle. Its shadows split it into separate forms, even though they are part of the same wall. The light of the sun is still one but now it seems to have multiplicity. The bodies are like the ramparts and the soul like the rays of the sun, as when it became attached to the numerous bodies it too became many souls. Rumi says metaphorically to take a catapult (effort and passion), and break these ramparts meaning make the bodies non-existent so that the soul attains its unity of form again.

Hence, to summarize:

- Just as Allah is One, so the spirit is one.
- He is Primary, so is the spirit.
- He is free of the constraints of matter and so is the spirit.

- Just as there is variety in the manifestation of the One True Being, so it is in the spirit.

So when these multiple manifestations are removed through focus and effort there remains no doubt about the knowledge and acquisition of the higher spiritual self.

Since this is a very delicate and complex concept for ordinary people, so Rumi quotes Prophet Muhammadﷺ to excuse himself from further discourse.

Prophet Muhammadﷺ said: "Speak to people according to their intellectual abilities."

These topics are like a steel sword that does not hesitate to cut; so if you lack depth of perception and understanding, it is best to withdraw. Misunderstanding these concepts could destroy faith (imaan). That is why, Rumi says, I have put the sword of this discussion in its sheath, that is, silence.

Then Rumi completes the tale of the vazir who killed himself after dividing the Christians into differing sects. There was bloodshed and turmoil among them but only one group was saved who honoured the name of Ahmedﷺ, as stated in the Gospel.

****

Go; strive after reality, O worshipper of form,
In as much as reality is the wing on form's body.
Consort with the followers of reality,
That you may both win the gift and be generous.

Beyond dispute, in this body the spirit devoid of reality
Is even as a wooden sword in the sheath.
While it remains in the sheath, it is valuable,
When it has come forth it is an implement for burning.
Do not take a wooden sword into the battle!
First see, in order that your trouble may not be wretched.
If it is made of wood, go, seek another;
And if it is a diamond, march forward joyously.
The sword is in the armoury of the saints:
To see them is for you the Elixir.

Rumi addresses the one occupied in worldly pursuits. When it has now been proven that spiritual life is the true reality so go forth and seek the attributes of spiritual excellence which are faith, morals, love, knowledge and sincerity. If you acquire worldly excellence which is devoid of spirituality then you are like a bird without wings, as you will not be able to soar.

Then Rumi explains that to attain spiritual perfection aspire for the company of the people of solitude and seekers of the path of spirituality. A soul in a body without spiritual excellence is like a wooden sword. As long as it is in its sheath it looks valuable but when it comes out it is only fit for firewood. Rumi warns that beware, do not take such a sword to the battlefield, that is, that Day of Judgement, as it will only be fit to burn. Find a sword that is beneficent and lavish like Almas, a diamond, meaning enhance your spiritual self. You will find this excellent sword in the arsenal of the friends of Allah so seek their company.

****

All the wise have said this same thing:

The wise man is a mercy to created beings.

If you would buy a pomegranate, buy laughing,

So that its laughter may give information as to its seeds.

Oh, blessed is its laughter, for through its mouth

It shows the heart, like a pearl from the casket of the spirit.

Unblessed was the laughter of the red tulip,

From whose mouth appeared the blackness of its heart.

The laughing pomegranate makes the garden laughing:

Companionship with men makes you one of the men.

Though you are a rock or marble,

You will become a jewel when you reach the friends of Allah.

Plant the love of the holy ones within your spirit;

Do not give your heart save to the love of them

whose hearts are glad.

Do not go to the neighbourhood of despair: there are hopes.

Go not in the direction of darkness: there are suns.

The heart leads you into the neighbourhood

of the friends of Allah;

The body leads you into the prison of water and earth.

Oh, give your heart food from one who is in accord with it;

Go, seek advancement from one who is advanced.

The company of the wise and holy is to be acquired and aspired for but there are certain conditions to be safe from malicious and false claimants of spiritual expertise. Just as the open pomegranate shows its beautiful kernels from the outside, in the same way a true spiritual guide will exhibit his inner moral excellence from his outside demeanour. He will have high ethics and enviable qualities. His company will fill the heart with agreeableness, peace, focus, love for Allah and His creation, and undesirability for the world.

Al-Quran (48:29) Muhammad is Allah's Apostle; and those who are [truly] with him are firm and unyielding towards all deniers of the truth, [yet] full of mercy towards one another. You can see them bowing down, prostrating themselves [in prayer], seeking favour with Allah and [His] goodly acceptance: their marks are on their faces, traced by prostration. (only relevant portion of verse quoted)

The Companions R.A. asked, "O Messenger of Allah! Which people with whom we sit are better?" The Prophet answered: "Those who make you remember Allah when they are seen, who increase your knowledge of good when they speak and whose deeds remind you of the hereafter."

After defining the friends of Allah, now Rumi goes on to talk about the blessings of their companionship. One moment spent in the company of the pure, devout and sincere is better than a hundred years of worship. Even if you are a like a mere rock, worthless and directionless, the attention of one who is on the true spiritual path will make you a priceless pearl. Place their love in your heart, but at the same time, do not get infatuated with any and all. Trust your heart and be aligned with it. Silence and stillness will give you guidance. Do not lose hope that you cannot find such true ones. Allah sends such sincere guides in every era. Do not lose yourself in worldly pursuits as that will create a curtain between you and the true ones. Keep walking on the path of truth and keep searching, your heart will lead you to such a spiritual mentor and guide.

Rumi counsels the seeker to give the heart its food, which is love and true knowledge. Hold the hand of the spiritually gifted; blessings can only be acquired from the blessed. The virtue of companionship is such that association with the honourable makes you honourable, and that of the dishonourable makes you dishonourable.

Prophet said: "The likeness of a righteous friend and an evil friend, is the likeness of a (musk) perfume seller and a blacksmith. As for the perfume seller, he may either bestow something on you, or you may purchase something from him, or you may benefit from his sweet smell. And as for the blacksmith, he may either burn your clothes, or you may be exposed to his awful smell."

****

Back to the Tale of the Vizier and his Plotting

The name of Mustafa was in the Gospel,

The chief of the prophets, the sea of purity.

There was mention of his characteristics and appearance;

There was mention of his warring and fasting and eating.

A party among the Christians, for the sake

of the Divine reward,

Whenever they came to that name and discourse,

Would bestow kisses on that noble name

And stoop their faces towards that beauteous description.

In this tragedy of which we have told,

That party were secure from tribulation and dread.

Secure from the mischief of the amirs and the vizier,

Seeking refuge in the protection of the Name of Ahmad ﷺ.

Their offspring also multiplied:

The Light of Ahmad ﷺ aided and befriended them.

And the other party among the Christians

Were holding the Name of Ahmad ﷺ in contempt.

They became contemptible and despised through conflicts

Caused by the evil-counselling and evil-plotting vizier.

Moreover, their religion and their law became corrupted

In consequence of the scrolls which set forth all corruptly.

The Name of Ahmad ﷺ gives such help as this,

So that how his Light keeps guard.

Since the Name of Ahmad ﷺ became an impregnable fortress,

What then must be the Essence of that trusted Spirit?

There were three groups of Christians.

One recognized the name of Muhammad ﷺ in their scriptures and paid due respect. They were saved from the vazir's plotting spiritually and physically, or were killed but unharmed spiritually.

Second were those that held his name in contempt (we seek refuge in Allahﷻ). They faced destruction both spiritually and physically.

Third group was one which neither disrespected nor respected. They remained in between the two.

Finally, Rumi says that if the name of Muhammadﷺ carries such strength then think of the Creator, how solidarity and closeness with the Supreme Being can save us from all the trials of the heart and soul.

Story IV:

Another Tyrannical King

A certain evil king, the same referred to in the chapter of the Quran, Al-Buruj (The Constellations), made up his mind to exterminate the Christian faith as that threatened his own power over people. With that in view, he set up a huge idol and issued commands that all who refused to worship it should be cast into the fire. During this happening, his officers seized a Christian woman with her baby, and as she refused to worship the idol, they threw her child into the fire. But the baby cried out to his mother, "Be not afraid as the fire has no power to burn me; it is like cool water". Hearing this, the rest of the Christians leapt into the fire and found the child was right; the fire did not burn them. The king reproached the fire for failing to do its job, but the fire replied that it was God's servant. It could only be used at His command. It then blazed up and consumed the king and all his followers.[xix]

Al-Quran (85:4-8) They destroy [but] themselves, they who would ready a (huge) pit of fire fiercely burning [for all who have attained to faith]! Lo! [With glee do] they observe that [fire], fully conscious of what they are doing to the believers, whom they hate for no other reason than that they believe in Allah, the Almighty, the One to whom all praise is due.

****

Another king, of the progeny of that Jew,

Addressed himself to the destruction of the people of Jesus.

If you desire information about this second outbreak,

Read the chapter of the Qur'an: By Heaven which has the signs.

This second king set foot in the evil way

That was originated by the former king.

Whoever establishes an evil tradition,

Towards him goes the curse of that every hour.

The righteous departed and their ways remained,

And from the vile there remained injustice and hate.

Until the Resurrection, the face of everyone following

those wicked men

Who comes into existence is turned towards that one.

Vein by vein is this sweet water and bitter water,

Flowing in creatures until the blast of the trumpet.

To the righteous is the inheritance of the sweet water.

What is that inheritance? We have caused to inherit the Book.

If you will consider, the supplications of the seekers

Are rays from the substance of prophethood.

The rays are circling with the substances:

The ray goes in the direction where that is.

The window-gleam runs round the house,

Because the sun goes from sign to sign of the zodiac.

This story is also about an evil king. The connection between the two stories could be that people of falsehood will always try to harm the people of Truth. They will do this at times spiritually, at times physically and at times both. Or that strength of faith is always a savior, just as in the previous story these people of faith were safe from the deception of the vazir whereas some of them were saved from being killed. Similarly, in this story people with a strong faith were protected from kneeling to the idol or being harmed by the fire.

Messenger of Allahﷺ said: Whosoever introduces a good practice in Islam, there is for him its reward and the reward of those who act upon it after him without anything being diminished from their rewards. And whosoever introduces an evil practice in Islam, will shoulder its sin and the sins of all those who will act upon it, without diminishing in any way their burden.

The one who did wrong invented that evil, and he will carry the burden of its curse and evil for each that follows him till the end of times.

Guidance and misguidance are embedded in all people. Whichever is in accordance with a person's nature he will accept that. The pious and seekers of Truth receive the inheritance of the Book of Allahﷻ.

Al-Quran (35:32) And so, We have bestowed this divine writ as a heritage unto such of Our servants as We chose: and among them are some who sin against themselves; and some who keep half-way [between right and wrong]; and some who, by Allah's leave, are foremost in deeds of goodness: [and] this, indeed, is a merit most high!

Their qualities of humility and obedience flow from the prophetic wisdoms. Sunbeams move around the pearl, just as sunlight infuses the house.

****

Now see what a plan this evil King contrived!
He set up an idol beside the fire,
Saying, "He that bows down to this idol is saved,
And if he bows not, he shall sit in the heart of the fire."
Inasmuch as he did not give due punishment to this idol of ego,
From the idol of his ego the other idol was born.
The idol of your ego is the mother of idols,
Because that idol is a snake, while this idol is a dragon.
The ego is iron and stone, while the idol is the sparks:
Those sparks are quieted by water.
How should the stone and iron be allayed by water?
How should a man, having these two, be secure?
The idol is the black water in a jug;
The ego is a fountain for the black water.
That sculptured idol is like the black torrent;
The idol-making ego is a fountain full of water for it.
A single piece of stone will break a hundred pitchers,
But the fountain is jetting forth water incessantly.

It is easy to break an idol, very easy;

To regard the ego as easily broken is folly, folly.

O son, if you seek the form of the ego,

Read the story of Hell with its seven gates.

Every moment an act of deceit,

and in every one of those deceits

A hundred Pharaohs are drowned together

with their followers.

Flee to the God of Moses and to Moses,

Do not from Pharaoh's quality spill the water of the Faith.

Lay your hand on the One﷽ and Ahmad﷽!

O brother, escape from the Bu Jahl of the body!

Rumi creates a profound personification of the egoistic self, showing how much more bigger, vile and dangerous it is than an idol. If the idol is the snake, the self is the dragon; if idol is the spark then the self is the iron and stone which create these sparks, and so on. The idol is the apparent evil which is easier to deal with than the hidden evil of the ego. To think that it is easy to curb and control the egoistic self is foolishness.

Just like hell has seven gates which open to all kinds of cruelty, vice and torture, in the same way the ego has thousands of gates of perversity and evil. In fact, the evil of Hell is the fruit of all these evils of the ego. Rumi then goes on to explain the way to success; attach yourself to the Lord of Moosa﷽ through faith and obedience. Hold on tenaciously to the One True Being﷽ and

Muhammadﷺ to find the real purpose of life and success in the Hereafter.

The ego is described as Abu Jahl who was one of the Meccan polytheist pagan leaders. He was one of the arch-enemies of Muhammadﷺ and the flag-bearer of opposition towards Islam and the early Muslims. Islam views him as having hatred and enmity to such an extent that Muhammadﷺ gave him the title of "The Pharaoh of my Ummah".

The Prophetﷺ said: "When Allah drowned Pharaoh, he said: I believe in the one in whom the children of Israel believe. Gabriel said: O Muhammad, if only you could have seen me while I was taking mud from the sea and filling his mouth, fearing lest the mercy of Allah should reach him."

****

That Jew brought to that idol a woman with her child
And the fire was blazing.
He took the child from her and cast it into the fire.
The woman took fright and withdrew her heart from her faith.
She was about to bow down before the idol
The child cried, "Truly, I am not dead.
Come in, O mother: I am happy here,
Although in appearance I am amidst the fire.
The fire is a spell that binds the eye for the sake of screening;
This is a Divine mercy which has raised its head from the collar.

Come in, mother, and see the evidence of God,

That you may behold the delight of God's elect.

Come in, and see water that has the semblance of fire;

From a world which is fire and has the semblance of water.

Come in, and see the mysteries of Abraham,

Who in the fire found roses and jasmine.

I was seeing death at the time of birth from you:

Painful was my dread of falling from you.

When I was born, I escaped from the narrow prison

Into a world of pleasant air and beautiful colour.

Now I deem the world to be like the womb,

Since in this fire I have seen such rest.

In this fire I have seen a world

Where every atom possesses the breath of Jesus.

Lo, a world apparently non-existent essentially existent,

While that world apparently existent has no permanence.

Come in, mother, by the right of motherhood:

See this fire, how it has no fieriness.

Come in, mother, for felicity is come;

Come in, mother, do not let fortune slip from your hand.

You have seen the power of that villain:

Come in, that you may see the power of God's grace.

It is out of pity that I am imploring you to come in,

For indeed such is my ecstasy that I have no care for you.

Come in and call the others also,

For the King has spread a table within the fire.

O true believers, come in, all of you:

Except for this sweetness ('adhbi) all is torment ('adhaab).

Oh, come in, all of you, like moths;
Into this fortune which has a hundred spring times."
He (the child) was crying amidst that multitude:
The souls of the people were filled with awe.
After that, the folk, men and women,
Cast themselves unthinkingly into the fire.
Without custodian, without being dragged, for love of the
Friend,
Because from Him is the sweetening of every bitterness—
Until it came to pass that the king's guards
Were holding back the people, saying, "Do not enter the fire!"
The Jew became black-faced and dismayed;
He became sorry and sick at heart,
Because the people grew more loving in their Faith
And more firm in surrendering of the body.
Thanks be to God, the Devil's plot caught him in its effort;
Thanks be to God, the Devil saw himself disgraced.
That which he was rubbing on the faces of those persons
Was all accumulated on the visage of that vile wretch.
He who was busy rending the garment of the people --
His own was rent, they were unhurt.

The child calls out to his mother to leave the world which has the face of water and comfort but in reality it is fire, and to come inside the fire where mysteries of Ibrahim are hidden. Outwardly it is fire, but inside it is the mercy of the Lord.

The decision to have Ibrahim (1813 – 1644 BCE) burned at the stake was affirmed by the temple priests and the king of

Babylon, Nimrod. The news spread like fire in the kingdom and people came from all over to watch the execution. A huge pit was dug up and a large quantity of wood was piled up. Then the biggest fire people ever witnessed was lit. The flames were so high up in the sky that even the birds could not fly over it for fear of being burnt themselves. Ibrahim's hands and feet were chained, and he was put in a catapult, ready to be thrown in. During this time, Angel Jibril came to him and said: "O Ibrahim! Is there anything you wish for?" Ibrahim could have asked to be saved from the fire or to be taken away, but he replied, "Allah is enough for me, He is the best guardian of my affairs."

Al-Quran (3:173) Those who have been warned by other people, "Behold, a group has gathered against you; so beware of them!" – whereupon this only increased their faith, so that they answered, "Allah is enough for us; and how excellent a guardian is He!

The catapult was released and Ibrahim was thrown into the fire. Allah then gave an order to the fire:

Al-Quran (21:69) [But] We said: O fire! Be coolness, and [a source of] inner peace for Abraham!

A miracle occurred; the fire obeyed and burned only his chains. Ibrahim came out from it as if he was coming out from a garden, peaceful, his face illuminated and not a trace of smoke on his clothes. People watched in shock and exclaimed: "Amazing! Ibrahim's God has saved him from the fire!"

The child says coming out from the dark womb he found the world vast and colourful. Now, after leaving that world and coming inside the fire, he could see another glorious world, the unseen world. Here each breath is life giving and immortal. These verses explain the confinement and limitation of this mortal world, and the limitlessness and permanence of the other world.

Al-Quran (29:64) For, [if they did, they would know that] the life of this world is nothing but a passing delight and a play - whereas, behold, the life in the Hereafter is indeed the only [true] life: if they but knew this!

The world seems existent and can be felt but it is mortal and will end soon. The other world is apparently non-existent but it has everlasting permanence.

Al-Quran (16:96) All that is with you is bound to come to an end, whereas that which is with Allah is everlasting. And most certainly shall We grant to those who are patient in adversity their reward in accordance with the best that they ever did.

Al-Quran (87:16-17) But no, [O people,] you prefer the life of this world, although the life to come is better and more enduring.

In this way, the Devil, meaning the King was doomed with his own plan to destroy the people of faith.

****

How the mouth remained crooked of a man who pronounced

The name of Mohammedﷺ insultingly.

He made his mouth mocking and called

the name of Ahmadﷺ in contempt:

His mouth remained misshapen.

He came back, saying, "Pardon me, O Mohammedﷺ,

O you to whom belong the gifts of knowledge.

In my foolishness I was ridiculing you,

I myself was an object of ridicule and deserving it."

When God wishes to tear apart the cover of anyone,

He turns his inclination towards reviling holy men.

When God wishes to hide the guilt of anyone,

He does not breathe a word of blame against the blameworthy.

When God wishes to help us,

He turns our inclination towards humble weeping.

Oh, happy the eye that is weeping for His sake!

Oh, fortunate the heart that is burned for His sake!

The end of every weeping is laughter at last;

The man who foresees the end is a blessed servant.

Wherever is flowing water, there is greenery:

Wherever are running tears, mercy is shown.

Be moaning and moist-eyed like the water-wheel

That green herbs may spring up from the courtyard of your
soul.

If you desire tears, have mercy on one who sheds tears;

If you desire mercy, show mercy to the weak.

Though this seems like a digression from the main story but is linked to the theme of how the King's plan backfired on him. Just as the one who took the name of Muhammadﷺ insultingly had his own mouth become crooked.

Rumi says Muhammadﷺ was mercy to mankind and forgave the man. If you want the mercy and beneficence of Allahﷻ then have mercy on the weak and those who shed tears of sorrow.

****

The king turned his face to the fire, saying, "O fierce-tempered one,
Where is your world-consuming natural disposition?
How are you not burning? What has become
of your specific property?
Or has your intention changed because of our fate?
You have no pity on the fire-worshipper.
How has he been saved who does not worship you?
Never, O fire, are you patient. How do you not burn?
What is it? Have you not the power?
Is this a spell, I wonder, that binds the eye or the mind?
How does the huge bonfire not burn?
Has some one bewitched you? Or is it magic,
Or is your unnatural behaviour from our fate?"
The fire said, "I am the same, I am fire.
Come in, that you may feel my heat.
My nature and element have not changed.
I am the sword of God and by His command I cut.

The Turcoman dogs kneel at the tent-door

Before the guest,

But if anyone having the face of a stranger pass by the tent

He will see the dogs rushing at him like lions.

I am not less than a dog in devotion,

Nor is God less than a Turcoman in life."

Rumi returns to the story. The king is addressing the fire in dismay and utter astonishment. He asks the fire what has changed its inherent nature. Is it magic or the king's misfortune?

The fire replies to the king that I'm the same fire. I'm the Lord's ﷻ sword that does not cut without His command; I am like the Turks' dogs, which do not bother the guests but in front of strangers they become fierce like lions.

****

If the fire of your nature makes you suffer pain,

It burns by the command of the Lord of Judgment ﷻ.

If the fire of your nature gives you joy,

The Lord of the Way ﷻ puts joy within.

When you feel pain, ask pardon of God ﷻ.

Pain, by command of the Creator ﷻ, is powerful.

When He pleases, pain itself becomes joy;

bondage itself becomes freedom.

Air and earth and water and fire are slaves.

With you and me they are dead, but with God☙ they are alive.

Before God☙, fire is always standing,

Writhing continually day and night, like a lover.
If you strike stone on iron, it leaps out.
It is by God's☙ command that it puts forth its foot.

Do not strike together the iron and stone of injustice,
For these two generate like man and woman.
The stone and the iron are indeed causes,
But look higher, O good man!
For this cause was produced by that cause.
When did a cause ever proceed from itself without a cause?
And those causes which guide the prophets on their way
Are higher than these causes.
That cause makes this cause operative;
sometimes, again, it makes it fruitless and ineffectual.
Minds are familiar with this cause,
But the prophets are familiar with those causes.

In the previous verses Rumi was talking about the apparent fire that is discernable by the naked eye. Now he talks about the spiritual fire that is burning within the soul. He says this fire too is under the command of its Lord☙ and whatever pain or joy you feel is only because of His decree. When you feel pain ask His forgiveness and He will, by the grace of his mercy, change the same pain into joy. The cause might remain the same but the effect will change, giving joy instead of pain. This could be because the wisdom behind it might come to light, or the hope of a greater reward by bearing could become the source of joy. The chains that bound could be the trigger for freedom.

Rumi says that not only fire, but all of creation, including the four elements are all subservient to Allah's commands. Most spiritual and scientific studies prove some kind of life for inanimate objects. Quran and Prophetic narrations also mention this.

Al-Quran (2:74) And yet, after all this, your hearts hardened and became like rocks, or even harder: for, behold, there are rocks from which streams gush forth; and, behold, there are some from which, when they are cleft, water issues; and, behold, there are some that fall down for awe of Allah. And Allah is not unmindful of what you do!

Al-Quran (59:21) Had We bestowed this Quran from on high upon a mountain, you would indeed see it humbling itself, breaking into pieces for awe of Allah. And [all] such parables We propound unto men, so that they might [learn to] think.

The Messenger of Allah said: Verily, the mountain of Uhud loves us and we love it.

Rumi talks about the worldly cause of any happening and the True Cause, which is from Allah. We can see the cause and effect in this world, but the reality is that the True Cause, Allah, controls the happening. The worldly cause might be present but it is His will that will allow its coming into effect or not. We perceive the worldly cause but only the Prophets are knowledgeable about the True Cause. Consequently, other pious souls find out about this Sacred Truth through their pure hearts full of generosity and compassion for all creation.

****

Had not the soul of the wind been informed by God,

How would it have distinguished amongst the people of 'Ad?

Hud drew a line round the believers;

The wind would become soft when it reached that place.

It was dashing to pieces in the

Air all who were outside of the line.

Likewise Shayban the shepherd

Used to draw a visible line round his flock

Whenever he went to the Friday service at prayer-time,

In order that the wolf might not raid and ravage there.

No wolf would go into that,

Nor would any sheep stray beyond that mark.

The wind of the wolf's and sheep's strong desire

Was blocked because of the circle of the man of God.

The waves of the sea, when they charged on by God's

command,

Discriminated the people of Moses from the Egyptians.

The earth, when the command came,

Drew Qarun with his gold and throne into its lowest depth.

The water and clay, when it fed on the breath of Jesus,

Spread wings and limbs, became a bird, and flew.

There was a wind storm at the time of Prophet Hud☐ due to Allah's wrath on the people of Ad.

In Islamic tradition, the people of Ad are believed to be among the first inhabitants of Arabia. They belong to what is known as the perished Arabs. Prophet Hud☐ was the great great grandson of Prophet Nooh☐. Prophet Hud☐ was sent in order to guide people back to the righteous path of God. Most of the citizens continued in their idolatrous ways, and Allah☬ destroyed the city in a great storm, saving Prophet Hud☐ and those who followed him.[xx]

Al-Quran (89:6) Have you not considered how your Lord dealt with Aad?

Rumi says the wind has a soul and that is how it distinguished between the wrong-doers and the pious when it was commanded by Allah☬ to destroy the city of Ad. Some would say this does not prove the wind's voluntary movement due to it having a soul; it could have simply been a forced movement due to Allah's☬ command. However, the drawing of the line by Prophet Hud☐ shows that the wind could distinguish between the righteous and the wrong-doers. If the wind had to only follow Allah's☬ command there was no need of a line.

Similarly, Shayban was a pious saint. He also drew a line which held back the wolf and stopped the sheep from crossing over.

These are further examples of how elements and non-living things too have a soul and choice, but only act on Allah's﷾ command, as does all creation.

Al-Quran (41:11) And He [it is who] applied His design to the skies, which were [yet but] smoke; and He [it is who] said to them and to the earth, Come [into being], both of you, willingly or unwillingly! - to which both responded, "We do come in obedience".

Al-Quran (26:63-66) Thereupon We inspired Moses thus: "Strike the sea with thy staff!" - where upon it parted, and each part appeared like a huge mountain. And We caused the pursuers to draw near to that place: and We saved Moses and all who were with him, and then We caused the others to drown.

Al-Quran (28:76) [NOW,] BEHOLD, Qarun was one of the people of Moses; but he arrogantly exalted himself above them - simply because We had granted him such riches that his treasure-chests alone would surely have been too heavy a burden for a troop of ten men or even more. When [they perceived his arrogance,] his people said to him: "Rejoice not [in thy wealth], for, verily, God does not love those who rejoice [in things vain]!

Al-Quran (5:110) {O Isa, son of Maryam} And when you created out of the clay, by My leave as the likeness of a bird, and you breathed into it and it became a (living) bird by my leave.

****

The king beheld these marvellous things;

He had nothing except mockery and denial.

His counsellors said, "Do not let go beyond limits,

Do not drive the horse of willfulness so far."

He handcuffed the counsellors and confined them;

He committed one injustice after another.

When the matter reached this pass, a shout came —

"Hold your foot, O villian! For Our vengeance is come."

After that, the fire blazed up forty feet high,

Became a ring, and consumed those Jews.

From fire was their origin in the beginning:

They went to their origin in the end.

That company was born of fire:

The way of each is towards the universal.

They were only a fire to consume the true believers:

their fire consumed itself like rubbish.

He whose mother is Hawiya (Hell-fire) —

Hawiya shall become his zavieh (direction).

The mother of the child is seeking it:

the source pursues the outcome.

If water is imprisoned in a tank, the wind sucks it up,

For it belongs to the original.

It sets it free; it drifts it away to its source,

Little by little, so that you do not see its drifting.

And our souls likewise this breath steals away,

Little by little, from the prison of the world.

The perfumes of our words ascend even unto Him,

Ascending from us wherever God knows.

Our breaths soar up with the choice,

As a gift from us, to the abode of everlastingness;

Then comes to us the reward of our speech,

A double thereof, as a mercy from the Glorious.

Then He causes us to go to good words like those,

That His servant may obtain of what he has obtained.

Thus do they ascend while His mercy descends continually:

May you never cease to keep that up!

So in the end, the evil king and his courtiers went back to their origin, which was fire.

Everything returns to its origin, on the principle of "like attracts like". To explain this, Rumi gives the example of the pious and their pure words, the remembrance of Allah, which rise up to the heavens, wherever He knows. There is a connection between the two, as virtuous words have an affinity with the holy place and Higher Acceptance. The speech is mentioned as "breath" because speech is formed from air, and this same air by coming in and going out of our bodies is breath.

Al-Quran (35:10) Whoever desires honor [through power] - then to Allah belongs all honor. To Him ascends good speech, and righteous work raises it. But they who plot evil deeds will have a severe punishment, and the plotting of those - it will perish.

When the good word rises up it gains acceptance from the Almighty and is remembered by Him for more favours. This, in turn, increases the slave's devotion and passion for obedience and worship.

Al-Quran (2:152) So remember Me, and I shall remember you; and be grateful unto Me, and deny Me not.

Hence, pious words and deeds ascend continually and in response, His mercy and guidance descends as both are complementary to one another in genre.

Al-Quran (55:60) Could the reward of good be anything at all but good?

****

The eyes of every set of people remain in the direction
Where one day they satisfied a delight.
That which bears a resemblance is a loan;
a loan is impermanent in the end.
Although the bird is delighted by a whistle,
It takes fright when it does not find its own kind.
Although the thirsty man is delighted by the mirage,
He runs away when he comes up to it, seeking water.
Although the needy are pleased with base gold,
Yet that is put to shame in the mint.
Beware! In case the imposture casts you out of the way;
In case false imagination cast you into the well.

The soul will attach itself to that with which it has affinity and kinship. If the focus is towards piety and the Almighty, it will lead to a life of obedience, service and worship. If the focus is towards the gratification of the ego and worldly gains it will lead a life of selfishness and lust.

Rumi is warning here about imposters on the path to Truth. Sometimes the seeker will find affinity with one who is not sincere and has only put on a garb of spirituality. His soul is one with deceit and he only walks this path for worldly gains. Just like the hunter blows a whistle with the sound of a bird to attract it so he can capture it in his snare, the bird thinks it is one of its own kind. When it comes close it realizes it's a trap and takes fright. Another example is of the mirage in a desert. The thirsty man is attracted to it but turns away in despair when he finds it to be just sand. Similarly, an impoverished man would be delighted to find artificial gold, without realizing it's not gold but only bears resemblance to gold. When it is heated in the mint its reality is exposed.

Rumi advises to beware and not get beguiled by false guides on your path to spirituality as you will lose the way.

Story V

The Lion and the Beasts

In the book of Kalila and Dimna[xxi] a story is told of a lion who oppressed all the beasts of the neighbourhood. He was in the habit of making constant raids upon them, to take and kill any of them he required for his daily food. At last, the beasts discussed this issue together, and agreed to give the lion one of themselves every day, to satisfy his hunger, if he, on his part, would stop attacking them all the time. The lion was initially unwilling to trust them, remarking that he always preferred to rely on his own effort. The beasts, however, succeeded in persuading him that it would be to his favour to trust providence and their word. To convince the lion that creations' exertions are in vain, they related the story of a man who got Prophet Solomon☈ to transport him to Hindustan to escape the angel of death he saw staring at him in the court. He was smitten by the angel the moment he got there as that was the place where he was meant to die.

Having made their point, the beasts started to fulfill their commitment to the lion. One day, it was the turn of the hare to be delivered as a victim to the lion. He requested the others to let him try out a strategy to outwit the lion. They scoffed at him as how could a small, silly beast like him trick the king of the jungle. The hare assured them that wisdom was from Allahﷻ, and He could choose weak things to conquer the strong if He so wished. At last they consented to let him try his luck.

The hare took his way slowly to the lion, and found him in rage for the delay. The hare said that he and another hare had set out together to appear before the lion but a fierce lion seized the hare and carried it off. On hearing this, the lion roared with anger and commanded the hare to show him this enemy that had trespassed on his area. He took him to a well, where the lion peered in and saw his own reflection and the hare next to him. Thinking he was seeing the foe with the stolen hare, he plunged in to attack and drowned. The hare sprang off and escaped.

The lion fell prey to his ego and false pride and so was punished. A small animal took him to his destruction.[xxii]

****

A number of beasts of chase in a pleasant valley
Were harassed by a lion.
Inasmuch as the lion was from ambush and carrying them away,
That grassland had become unpleasant to them all.
They made a plot: they came to the lion, saying,
"We will keep you full-fed by means of an allowance.
Do not go after any prey beyond your allowance,
In order that this grass may not become bitter to us."

> **"Yes," said he, "If I see good faith, not fraud,**
>
> **For often have I seen frauds from Zayd and Bakr.**
>
> **I am done to death by the cunning and fraud of men.**
>
> **I am bitten by the sting of snake and scorpion.**
>
> **Worse than all men in fraud and spite**
>
> **Is the man of the ego lying in wait within me.**
>
> **My ear heard, 'The believer is not bitten',**
>
> **And adopted the saying of the Prophetﷺ with heart and soul."**

Zayd and Bakr, often used Arabic names, means I have seen the trickery and vile of all sorts of people.

Rumi transitions here to the egoistic self as is his way in the whole Mathnavi, and says that the most damage and wickedness is inculcated by the ego that is in a constant state of ambush to destroy a man's body and soul.

Prophetﷺ said: "The believer does not allow himself to be stung twice from the same hole."

The bite by a snake is used as a metaphor to mean get hurt, cheated or suffer damage in any way. This Hadith means that while it is possible for a believer to suffer if he is taken unaware, the same thing should not be allowed to happen twice. He should always be careful so that he would not commit the same mistake, or be in the same situation of overlooking real danger, more than once.

Even though the words of the Prophetic narration are general, but Islam places greater emphasis on the damage inflicted on a man's spirituality. Hence, it would then mean that if a believer perceives that the company or association of a certain person, or a situation is detrimental to his spiritual growth or his morality, then he should avoid it. As far as worldly matters are concerned, another Prophetic narration gives a different perspective.

Prophetﷺ said: "The believer is simple and noble." In this hadith it means that one who is pious is of a soft disposition and he trusts everyone, which is why he is so easily deceived by people. He constantly remembers the Hereafter, believes in the inherent goodness of all men, and forgives those who hurt or deceive him. He keeps in mind the reward for forgiving in the Hereafter, so he does not take revenge upon anybody.

✳✳✳✳✳✳✳✳✳

> **They all said: "O knowing sage, let precaution alone.**
> **It is of no avail against the Divine decree.**
> **In precaution is conflict, agitation and suffering:**
> **Go, put your trust in God: trust in God is better.**
> **Do not grapple with Destiny, O fierce and furious one,**
> **Lest Destiny also pick a quarrel with you.**
> **One must be dead in presence of the decree of God,**
> **So that no blow may come from the Lord of the daybreak."**

These verses exhort putting complete trust on predestination. What is the ruling for planning and exercising prudence to acquiring one's purpose? According to Maulana Ashraf Ali

Thanvi, as mentioned in Kaleedi Mathnavi there are certain aspects and rulings to this question.

1. Planning has two aspects; beneficial, secondly, permissible.

2. Planning will be beneficial when it is in accordance with predestination, otherwise it will be unfruitful.

3. Permissible has two angles.

One is the belief that planning and acquiring the means is the ultimate cause of success or failure. This is unlawful according to the Islamic law. The people on the True Path believe planning and acquiring means are only effectual along with predestination. They do not have complete power within themselves.

Second perspective is to acquire the means for any purpose. Here the purpose needs to be considered. This has three dimensions.

a) The purpose is religious or worldly, permissible or unlawful. If it is worldly and unlawful religiously and morally, then acquiring the means for it is absolutely impermissible.

b) If it is permissible and for religious purpose, then it should be considered that is it obligatory or desirable. If it is an obligatory act, then acquiring the means for it is obligatory and if it is desirable, then acquiring its means will also be desirable.

c) If the purpose is worldly gains, and permissible religiously and morally, then it should be considered if it is necessary or unnecessary. If it is necessary and if acquiring the means would make its happening definite, then it is obligatory to acquire the means. If its happening is uncertain, then it is permissible for the weak to acquire the means but for the strong, though permissible, to leave it is better.

4. If that purpose for worldly gains is detrimental religiously and morally then it is illegal to acquire the means for it to happen. If not detrimental, then allowed but to leave it is better.

All these different aspects and rulings explain when complete reliance on predestination is permissible or non-permissible, and when acquiring the means for any purpose is permissible or non-permissible.

****

How the lion upheld the superiority of exertion and acquisition along with trust in God and resignation.

"Yes," he said; "If trust in God is the guide,

Then means too is the Prophet's﷽ tradition (sunnah).

The Prophet﷽ said with a loud voice, 'While trusting in Allah﷽,

tie the knee of your camel to the post.'

Be mindful to the signification of 'The earner is beloved of God'.

Through trusting in God do not become neglectful

as to the means."

Exertion and effort make you the beloved of Allah and save from the harmful effects of laziness and sloth. This has been emphasized both in the Quran and Prophetic narrations.

Al-Quran (29:6) Hence, whoever strives hard does so only for his own good: for, verily, Allah does not stand in need of anything in all the worlds!

Al-Quran (29:69) As for those who strive hard in Us (Our Cause), We will surely guide them to Our Paths. And verily, Allah is with the doers of good.

****

<u>**How the beasts preferred trust in God to exertion.**</u>

There is no work better than trust in God.

What, indeed, is dearer than resignation?

Often do they flee from affliction to affliction;

Often do they recoil from the snake to the dragon.

He locked the door while the foe was in the house.

The plot of Pharaoh was a story of this sort.

That vengeful man (Pharoah) slew

hundreds of thousands of babes,

While the one he was searching after (Moosa﷼) was in his

house.

Since in our eyesight there is much defect, go,

Let your own sight wipe out in the sight of the Friend.

His sight for ours — what a goodly recompense!

In His sight you will find the whole object of your desire.

He who gives rain from heaven is also able,

From His mercy, to give us bread."

Reference to the story of Moosa⁣ in the Quran:

Al-Quran (28:8) And [some of] Pharaoh's household found [and spared] him (Moosa⁣): for [We had willed] that he becomes an enemy unto them and [a source of] grief, seeing that Pharaoh and Haman and their hosts were sinners indeed!

Al-Quran (28:9) Now the wife of Pharaoh said: "A joy to the eye [could this child Moosa be] for me and you! Slay him not: he may well be of use to us, or we may adopt him as a son!" And they had no presentiment [of what he was to become].

All these verses have one central theme: Means were only created for the weak of faith. There is no exertion better than faith in predestination.

✳✳✳✳✳✳✳✳✳

<u>How the lion again pronounced exertion to be superior along with trust in God.</u>

"Yes," said the lion; "But the Lord of His servants

Set a ladder before our feet.

Step by step must we climb towards the roof.

To be passive here is foolish hopes.

You have feet; why do you make yourself out to be lame?

You have hands; why do you conceal the fingers?

When the master put a spade in the slave's hand,

His purpose was made known to him without speaking.

Hand and spade alike are His implicit signs;

Thinking upon the end are His explicit declarations.

When you take His signs to heart,

You will devote your life to fulfilling that indication.

He will give you many hints of mysteries;

He will remove the burden from you and give you authority.

Do you bear? He will cause you to be borne.

Do you receive? He will cause you to be received.

If you accept His command, you will become the spokesman;

If you seek union, thereafter you will become united.

Freewill is the effort to thank for His beneficence;

Your fatalism is the denial of that beneficence.

Thanksgiving for the power increases your power;

Fatalism takes the gift out of your hand.

Your fatalism is sleeping on the road: do not sleep!

Sleep not, until you see the gate and the holy place!

Beware! Do not sleep, O inconsiderate fatalist,

Save underneath that fruit-laden tree,

So that every moment the wind may shake the boughs

And shower upon the sleeper dessert

and provision for the journey.

If you are putting trust in God, put trust as regards work;

Sow, then rely upon the Almighty."

Fatalism is of two kinds. One where the person believes man has no control or authority, whether potent or weak, over his affairs. He is completely subservient to predestination. This is undesirable and unlawful according to the Islamic law. The true scholars claim it invalid according to the Quran and Sunnah. This belief leads to decline or abandonment of good deeds, as well as fearlessness and negligence in following egoistic desires, because of the justification of innocence and helplessness.

Second fatalism is the observance of the dominance of Allah's power. In spite of knowing that man has some power and control over his actions, he considers himself weak in the presence of the Almighty. Even though he does not negate his own power, but regards it as non-existent compared to the might of Allah. This is desirable fatalism and the way of the sincere believer. Achieving this state increases and effectuates obedience and disregard of all desires of the self that go against the will of the One True Being.

Rumi says, "Don't sleep!" Sleep here represents fatalism. Rumi says it is only your ego that is driving you to sloth and laziness in your exertion.

Exert yourself on the path of seeking the truth and acquiring the means, to live a life according to the will of the Almighty. Become a fatalist after you reach that point of knowledge and observance of the might of Allah, meaning the door of the Holy Place.

Assume desirable fatalism once you have reached a level of closeness and discernment of Truth through exertion and effort. Then you will be like the sleeper upon whom the fruits of the grace and mercy of the Almighty☀ will shower without effort and exertion.

Put your faith in effort and of acquiring the means to achieve your passion and livelihood, but believe that result is only dependent on the will of the Almighty☀.

****

How the beasts once more asserted the superiority of complete trust in God to exertion.

They all lifted up their voices with him, saying,
"Those materialistic ones who sowed means,
Countless and countless of men and women —
Why, then, did they remain deprived of fortune?
From the beginning of the world countless of generations
Have opened a hundred mouths, like dragons.
Those clever people devised plots
That the mountain thereby was torn up from its foundation.
The Glorious described their plots:
That the tops of the mountains might be moved thereby.
Except the portion which came to pass in eternity,
Nothing showed its face from their scheming and doing.
They all fell from plan and act;

The acts and decrees of the Maker remained.

O noble one; do not regard work as anything but a name!
O cunning one, do not think that exertion is anything

but a vain fancy!"

Al-Quran (14:46) And [this retribution will befall all evildoers because] they devise that false imagery of theirs - and all their false imagery is within God's knowledge. [And never can the blasphemers prevail against the truth - not] even if their false imagery were so (well devised and so powerful) that mountains could be moved thereby.

Al-Quran (26:146 - 149) "Do you think that you will be left secure [forever] in the midst of what you have here and now? Amidst [these] gardens and springs and fields, and [these] palm-trees with slender spathes and that you will [always be able to] carve dwellings out of the mountains with [the same] great skill?

****

How Azrael, the Angel of Death, looked at a certain man, & how that man fled to the palace of Prophet Solomon

One forenoon a freeborn man arrived
And ran into Prophet Solomon's hall of justice,
His countenance pale with anguish and both lips blue.
Then Prophet Solomon said, "Good sir, what is the matter?"
He replied, "Angel Azrael cast on me such a look,
so full of wrath and hate."

"Come," said the king, "What do you desire now? Ask!"
"O protector of my life," said he, "Command the wind
To bear me from here to India.
Maybe, when your slave is there his life will be saved."
Lo, the people are fleeing from poverty;
hence are they a mouthful for greed and expectation.
The fear of poverty is like that terror;
Know you that greed and striving are India.
He commanded the wind to bear him quickly
Over the water to the uttermost part of India.
Next day, at the time of conference and meeting,
Prophet Solomon said to Angel Azrael:
"Did you look with anger on that Moslem
in order that he might wander far from his home?"
Angel Azrael said, "When did I look angrily?
I saw him as I passed by, in astonishment,
For Allahﷻ had commanded me, saying,

'Listen, to-day, take his spirit in India.'
From wonder I said, if he has a hundred wings,
It is a far journey for him to be in India."
In like manner judge all the affairs of this world
And open your eyes and see!
From whom shall we flee? From ourselves? Oh, absurdity!
From whom shall we take away? From Allahﷻ? Oh, crime!

Rumi transitions from the main story, as per habit, to express the principle that experience and intellect, when in conflict with predestination can never triumph. The man's fear of death is the metaphor for fear of poverty and the like, and India represents his greed and exertion. However much he planned and executed, it was to no avail. Similarly, all the exertion in the world cannot save one from poverty if that is predestined.

Rumi emphasizes that to run from destiny is to get trapped in destiny.

****

How the lion again expounded the advantages of exertion.

"Yes," said the lion; "But at the same time

Consider the exertions of the prophets and the true believers.

God, exalted is He, flourished their exertion

And what they suffered of oppression and heat and cold.

Their plans were excellent in all circumstances:

Everything done by a good man is good.

Their snares caught the Heavenly bird,

All their deficiencies turned to increment."

O master, exert yourself so long as you can

In the way of the prophets and saints!

Endeavour is not a struggle with Destiny,

Because Destiny itself has laid this upon us.

I am an infidel if anyone has suffered loss a single moment

In the way of faith and obedience.

Your head is not broken: do not bandage this head.

Exert yourself for a day or two, and laugh unto everlasting!

The prophets' and true believers' efforts helped them attain lofty stations of the Everlasting abode.

This is in answer to the animals' claim that effort is a struggle with destiny. The lion says striving is not opposition to destiny, in fact, it has been decreed through destiny. Never has anyone suffered loss on account of striving in the way of Allah﷽. To stop striving to attain excellence is just like wrapping up our head in a bandage when there is no injury. Rumi, through the lion's dialogue exhorts effort, as this will lead to everlasting joy.

****

An evil resort sought he that sought this world;
A good state sought he that sought the world to come.
Plots for gaining this world are worthless;
Plots for renouncing this world are inspired.
The plot is that he digs a hole in his prison;
If he blocks up the hole, that is a foolish plot.
This world is the prison, and we are the prisoners:
Dig a hole in the prison and let yourself out!

From the previous verses one might take a general meaning of effort and striving. To clarify this misconception, Rumi says that the purpose is to guide towards the desire and striving for the Everlasting abode rather than for the worldly desires. To strive for this world is to strive for futility, whereas striving for the Everlasting abode is the real purpose.

The Prophetﷺ said: A place in Paradise as small as a bow is better than all that on which the sun rises and sets (i.e. all the world).

Messenger of Allahﷺ said: Going out in the way of Allahﷻ in the morning or in the evening (will merit a reward) better than the world and all that is in it.

Messenger of Allahﷺ said: The world is a prison for the believer and Paradise for the disbeliever.

****

What is this world? To be forgetful of God;
It is not merchandise, silver, weigh-scales and women.
As regards the wealth that you carry for religion's sake,
"How good is righteous wealth!" the Prophetﷺ recited.

Water in the boat is the ruin of the boat,
Water underneath the boat is a support.
Since he cast out from his heart wealth and possessions,
On that account Prophet Solomon did not
call himself but "poor."
The sealed jar, in rough water,
Floated on the water because of its air-filled heart.
When the wind of poverty is within,
He rests at peace on the surface of the water of the world.
Although the whole of this world is his kingdom,
In the eye of his heart the kingdom is nothing.
Therefore stopper and seal the mouth of your heart,

And fill it from the inward ventilator.

Exertion is a reality, and medicine and disease are realities;

The skeptic in his denial of exertion practices exertion.

After strongly encouraging the reader to renounce this world and all that is in it, Rumi now clarifies the reality of this world. This world is the state of living before death. If it takes you to spend your life and wealth in the way of Allah﷾ and goodness, then it is desirable. If it takes you to greed and lust, and forgetfulness of Allah﷾ then it is shame and dishonor.

The Messenger of Allahﷺ said: When Allah wants good for a slave, He puts him in action. It was said: "How does he put him in action O Messenger Of Allah?" He said: "By making him meet up with the righteous deeds before death".

Allah's Messengerﷺ ascended the pulpit and said: "Nothing worries me as to what will happen to you after me, except the temptation of worldly blessings which will be bestowed on you." Then he mentioned the worldly pleasures. He started with the one (i.e. the blessings) and took up the other (i.e. the pleasures). A man got up saying, "O Allah's Messenger! Can the good bring about evil?" The Prophetﷺ remained silent and we thought that he was being inspired divinely, so all the people kept silent with awe. Then the Prophetﷺ wiped the sweat off his face and asked, "Where is the present questioner?" "Do you think wealth is good?" he repeated thrice, adding, "No doubt, good produces nothing but good. Indeed it is like what grows on the banks of a stream which either kills or nearly kills the grazing animals because of gluttony except the animal which eats till it gets satisfied and then stands in the sun and defecates and urinates and again starts grazing. This worldly property is sweet vegetation. How excellent the wealth of the Muslim is, if it is collected through legal means and is spent in Allah's cause and on orphans, poor people and travelers. But he who does not take it legally is like an eater who is never satisfied and his wealth will be a witness against him on the Day of Resurrection."

Rumi explains metaphorically that the ship is like the heart and the water like the world. As long as the heart is devoid of the world, empty except for the love of the Almighty, worldly strength can help man attain everlasting glory. If the heart is filled with love of this world and all that it contains, then it leads to his destruction in both the worlds.

Prophet Solomon, in spite of his wealth and glory, never considered himself anything but powerless in front of the Almighty. In his letter to the Queen of Sheba, he didn't add the title of king before his name and signed off simply as Solomon. This was because he had emptied his heart of wealth and title. This shows that the true meaning of worldly love is to have the world possess man and his heart, rather than man possessing the kingdom and wealth to dispose for the good of all.

The air-filled heart and the wind of poverty are metaphors for the heart empty of all except the love of Allah. A heart such as this lives in peace, and deals with the worldly affairs with joy and goodness. He cannot get drowned by the stormy waves of worldly desires.

Seal your heart, don't let the world in and fill it with the air of Allah's greatness.

To summarize the lion's case for struggle and effort, Rumi says strive in this world for goodness so you can gain knowledge of the mysteries of Allah. You will see the wisdom behind the connection between means and gains. Striving and effort are the Truth and the medicine of Truth is the pain of the truth. When you have pain you go in search of medicine. Paradoxically, the unbeliever and skeptic, to deny this universal truth, exerts effort and struggles to prove his point!

****

The lion gave many proofs in this style,
So that those fatalists became tired of answering.
They made bonds with the furious lion,
That he should incur no loss in this bargain.
The daily ration should come to him without trouble,
And that he should not need to make a further demand.
Day by day the one on whom the lot fell
Would run to the lion as a cheetah.
When this cup came round to the hare, the hare cried out,
"Why, how long are we to endure injustice?"
The company said to him: "All this time
We have sacrificed our lives in faith and loyalty.
Do not seek to give us a bad name, O rebellious one!

Lest the lion be aggrieved, go, go! Quick! Quick!"

"O friends," said he, "Grant me a respite,

That by my cunning you may escape from trickery,

That by my cunning your lives may be saved

And remain as a heritage to your children."

Every prophet amidst the peoples used to call them

After this manner to a place of deliverance,

For he had seen from Heaven the way of escape,

In sight he was contracted like the pupil of the eye.

Men regarded him as small like the pupil;

None attained to the greatness of the pupil.

Rumi transitions from the main story to explain how all prophets came to this world to guide people to the best way. They had, through their enhanced spiritual prowess and the strength of their observation, understood the deeper truth about human existence. The people, however, saw them as regular people, or maybe even less in stature and size just as the pupil of the eye. It is so small in size and yet all our sight and perception depends on it. What a beautiful analogy!

****

The company said to him: "O donkey, listen!

Keep yourself within the measure of a hare!

Eh, what brag is this --- which your betters

Never brought into their minds?

You are strange, or Destiny is pursuing us;

Else, how is this speech suitable to one like you?"

The hare said: " O friends, God gave me inspiration;

To a weakling there came a strong judgment."

That which God taught to the bees

Is not to the lion and the wild ass.

It makes houses of juicy sweets;

God opened to it the door of that knowledge.

That which God taught to the silkworm —

Does any elephant know such a device?

Adam created of earth, learned knowledge from God;

Knowledge shot beams up to the Seventh Heaven.

He broke the name and fame of the angels,

To the confusion of that one who is in doubt concerning God.

He made the ascetic of so many thousand years

A muzzle for that young calf, that he might not be

Able to drink the milk of knowledge of religion,

And that he might not roam around that lofty castle.

The sciences of the followers of sense became a muzzle,

So that he might not receive milk from that sublime knowledge.

Into the blood-drop of the heart there fell an essence

Not given to the seas and skies.

The hare gives various examples to illustrate the point that inspiration has no relationship with strength or weakness of form.

Al-Quran (16:68) And [consider how] thy Sustainer has inspired the bee: "Prepare for thyself dwellings in mountains and in trees, and in what [men] may build [for thee by way of hives].

Adam was made of clay which is by nature dark and lowly but through the knowledge and inspiration from Allah he lighted up the heavens and the earth. Satan, a devout and ascetic for thousands of years, is made of fire which is bright and lofty, but was reduced to the level of a calf in his foolishness and ignorance. A muzzle is tied around the calf's mouth so that it can't drink from the cow's milk. Metaphorically, a muzzle was tied around Satan's intellect so that he could not avail of the knowledge and light of Adam.

In the same way, those intellectuals whose knowledge does not reach their heart and soul are like the calf with a muzzle on its mouth; just as it can't get its milk so their superficial knowledge is like the muzzle which deprives them of the light of True Knowledge.

A drop of blood in a small organ such as the heart contains the essence of life, intellect and wisdom the likes of which has not been granted to huge oceans, skies and mountains. So again he proves that size and strength have no correlation to inspiration and magnificence. As Rumi himself says elsewhere:

> You are not a drop in the ocean; You are the
> entire ocean in a drop.

****

How long form? After all, O form-worshipper,
Has your reality-lacking soul not escaped from form?

If a human being were a man in virtue of form,
Ahmad﷽ and Bu Jahl would be just the same.

Rumi asks a rhetorical question here to present the case against form verses soul. Form is only the outward manifestation of man. The hidden soul is the true essence of humanity. He gives the example of Prophet Muhammad (Ahmad) ﷺand Abu Jahl, the greatest enemy of Islam. Though both possessed the human image outwardly, but inwardly their souls were as apart as the earth and the sky. Prophet Muhammadﷺ was sent down as a mercy to the worlds.

Al-Quran (21:107) And [thus, O Prophet,] We have sent you as [an evidence of Our] mercy towards all the worlds.

Abu Jahl was known to be one of the arch-enemies and the flag-bearer of opposition towards Islam and the early Muslims. He oppressed the poor and weak. Abu Jahl was infamous for his ruthless attitude toward orphans as well. His wealth and position made him arrogant and merciless. Islam views him as having malevolence and enmity to such an extent that Prophet Muhammadﷺ gave him the title of "The Pharaoh of this Ummah".

Muhammadﷺ said: He who calls Abu Jahl 'Abu Hakam' (his actual name meaning father of wisdom) has made a serious mistake. He should seek forgiveness from Allah for this.

When Abu Jahl heard that a man had become a Muslim, if he was a man of social importance and had relations to defend him, he reprimanded him and poured scorn on him, saying, 'You have forsaken the religion of your father who was better than you. We will declare you a blockhead and brand you as a fool, and destroy your reputation.' If he was a merchant he said, 'We will boycott your goods and reduce you to beggary.' If he was a person of no social importance, he beat him and incited people against him. Therefore, many converted slaves had to suffer the extreme savagery of Abu Jahl.[xxiii]

Abu Jahl worshipped and prostrated before stones (idols) whereas stones prostrated before Prophet Muhammad.

Before the beginning of his prophethood, God's Noble Messenger was travelling towards Damascus to trade together with his uncle Abu Talib and some of the Quraysh. They rested when they came near the church of Bahira the monk. Bahira, who was a hermit and did not mix with people, suddenly came out. He saw Muhammad the Trustworthy among the caravan, and said: "He is the Lord of the World; he will be a prophet." Abu Talib asked: "How do you know?" The holy monk replied: "I saw a small cloud over the caravan as you were coming. When you sat down, the cloud moved toward him and cast its shadow over him. I also saw trees and rocks prostrate themselves before him, which they do only before prophets."

On the conquest of Makkah, there were three hundred and sixty idols around the Ka'ba, fixed with lead to the stone. That day, the Noble Prophet pointed to each of the idols in turn with a stick he was holding curved like a bow, saying, **"The Truth has arrived**

and falsehood has perished; indeed, falsehood is ever bound to perish." (Al-Quran 17:81) Whichever one he pointed to, it fell down. If he pointed to the face of the idol, it fell backwards; otherwise, it fell on its face. Thus, they all toppled over and fell to the ground.

****

The painting on the wall is like Adam:
See from the form what thing in it wants.
The spirit is wanting in that resplendent form;
Go, seek that essence rarely found!
The heads of all the lions in the world were laid low
When they gave a hand to the dog of the Companions.
What loss does it suffer from that abhorred shape,
In as much as its spirit was plunged in the ocean of light?

A mere picture of man is lacking in the real essence which is the soul. Rumi exhorts to stop looking at form and find the real heart and soul of humanity.

The dog of the Companions of the Cave became loftier in status than the lions by his mere companionship with the beloveds of Allah and his mention in the Holy Book. His lesser form does not negate the spiritual light within him.

Al-Quran (18:18) And you would have thought them awake, while they were asleep. And We turned them on their right and on their left sides, and their dog stretching forth his two forelegs at the entrance [of the Cave or in the space near to the entrance of the Cave (as a guard at the gate)]. Had you looked at them, you would certainly have turned back from them in flight, and would certainly have been filled with awe of them.

****

This topic has no end. Pay attention!
Listen to the story of the hare.
Sell your foolish ear and buy another ear,
For the senseless ear will not apprehend this discourse.
Go, behold the foxy tricks played by the hare;
Behold how the hare made a plot to catch the lion.
Knowledge is the seal of the kingdom of Solomon;
The whole world is form, and knowledge is the spirit.
Because of this virtue, the creatures of the seas
And those of mountain and plain are helpless before man.
Of him the leopard and lion are afraid, like the mouse;
From him the crocodile of the great river
is in paleness and agitation.
From him peri and demon took to the shores:
Each took abode in some hiding-place.

Rumi says this topic of form and soul is too deep for your mindless listening. You need to open your spiritual sense of listening to be able to comprehend the true moral of this story.

As the story revolves around the wisdom of the hare, so Rumi again transcends to the virtue of knowledge.

Seal of Prophet Solomon﷩ refers to his famous ring. Rumi says the ring was only the outward form. The real essence of the might of his kingdom was the knowledge and wisdom granted to Prophet Solomon﷩.

Peri is a mythical superhuman being in Persian mythology, originally represented as evil but subsequently as a good or graceful genie or fairy.

Just as a living body is an indication of the soul, so are knowledge and wisdom signs of the characteristics of Allahﷻ. A man without wisdom and knowledge is like a body without a soul.

****

Man has many a secret enemy;

The cautious man is a wise one.

Hidden creatures, evil and good;

At every instant their blows are striking on the heart.

If you go into the river to wash yourself,

A thorn in the water pierces your skin.

Although the thorn is hidden low in the water,

You know it is there, since it is pricking you.

The pricks of inspirations and temptations

Are from thousands of beings, not from one.

Wait for your senses to be transformed, so that

You may see them, and the difficulty may be solved.
So that you know whose words you have rejected
And whom you have made your captain.

The previous verses talked about the apparent enemies of man that, though much stronger in body, are fearful of man due to his intellect.

Now Rumi talks about the virtual enemies of the spirit from whom the wise man takes caution. Just as there are evil influences from Satan, ego, etc, on our heart and soul, in the same way there are benevolent influences too from the angels and other favourable forces. We cannot see them with our naked eye but can feel their effects on our heart.

Al-Quran (50:27) Man's other self will say: O our Sustainer! It was not I that led his conscious mind into evil [nay,] but it had gone far astray [of its own accord]!

The Messenger of Allahﷺ said: To everyone among you a companion from among the jinn has been assigned. They said, "Even you, O Messenger of Allah?' He said, "Even me, but Allahﷺ helped me with him and he became Muslim (or: and I am safe from him), so he only enjoins me to do that which is good."

(According to another report, "… There is assigned to him a companion from among the jinn and a companion from among the angels.")

Rumi gives an example from daily life of when a thorn pricks us to explain how we are affected by something and know its presence even though we can't see it.

Patience or effort will open the mystery of this hidden companion. Your sense of knowledge will deepen and increase either through patience till death or through your effort and striving so that the mysteries of the universe are opened upon your heart and soul. Then you will find out whose counsel you rejected and whose you accepted; The devil's or the angel's or vice versa.

****

Afterwards they said, "O nimble hare, communicate
what is in your apprehension.
O you, who has grappled with a lion, declare the
plan which you have thought of.
Counsel gives perception and understanding:
the mind is helped by minds.
The Prophet said, ' O adviser, take counsel,
for he whose counsel is sought is trusted.'
He (hare) said, "One ought not to say forth
every secret: sometimes the even number
Turns out to be odd, and sometimes
the odd number to be even."
If from guilelessness you breathe words to a mirror,
The mirror at once becomes dim to us.

Do not move your lip in explanation of these three things,
(Namely) concerning your path and your gold and your belief;
For to these three there is many an adversary and foes
Standing in wait for you when he knows.
And if you tell one or two, farewell: every secret
That goes beyond the two is published abroad.
If you tie two or three birds together, they will remain
On the ground, imprisoned by grief.

The animals finally give up the argument and ask the hare to discuss his plan with them as consultation has wisdom and is from the people of knowledge. The Quran and the Prophet Muhammadﷺ encourage Muslims to decide their affairs in consultation with those who will be affected by that decision.

Since consultation has a significant effect in resolving problems, Allahﷻ orders the Prophetﷺ to consult with others in finding solutions.

Al-Quran (3:159) And make counsel with them in the affair; so when you have decided, then place your trust in Allah; surely Allah loves those who trust.

It is the praiseworthy life style of a successful believer, the religious and faithful people, whom Allahﷻ describes in the following manner:

Al-Quran (42:38) And those who respond to their Lord, keep up prayer, who consult among themselves, and who give out (to the poor) part of what we have given them.

Companion of the Prophet Abu Huraira reported: I never saw anyone consult his companions more often than the Messenger of Allah.

The Messenger of Allah said: The one who is consulted is in a position of trust.

The hare refuses to divulge his strategy saying consultation is a very good thing but not in all circumstances. Sometimes there are too many opposing views and it clouds our judgement, explaining through the metaphor of the mirror.

From one or two, the secret is then shared with others, and remains a secret no more. So be secretive of your vision, wealth and beliefs, as these are often the most in danger of being sabotaged. Just like birds tied together your secret will remain safe till you speak about it; untie them and they are not in your control anymore, they fly off.

****

They hold a consultation well-disguised and mingled,

In its significance, with that which casts error.

The Prophet used to take counsel, vaguely,

And they (the companions) would answer

him without knowledge.

He would speak his opinion in a hidden parable,

In order that the adversary might not know foot from head.

He would receive his answer from him,

While the other would not catch the smell of his question.

Rumi says that from the previous verses it should not be taken to mean that consultation in matters of secrecy is not advised. The habit of consultation is very important but should be preferably done in such a way that the secret remains a secret. Counsel should be sought such that the real matter remains vague to the counsellor, so that the advice can be pondered and acted upon and yet the real issue is hidden.

The Prophetﷺ would use suppositions and metaphors to ask advice so that others would be able to give their opinions and yet remain ignorant of the reality.

****

He that searches after wisdom becomes a fountain of wisdom;
He becomes independent of acquisition and means.
The guarding tablet becomes a Guarded Tablet;
His understanding becomes enriched by the Spirit.
When a man's understanding has been his teacher,
After this, the understanding becomes his pupil.
The understanding says, like Gabriel,
"O Ahmadﷺ, if I take one step, it will burn me;

Leave me, go on: this is my limit,
O sultan of the soul!"

Initially, man's intellect is his guide on the path to knowledge. He preserves the acquired knowledge on the tablet of his heart and mind but then he himself becomes a source of knowledge through his seeking. Inspiration descends on his heart directly, and he gains knowledge and perception that is beyond the cognizance of his intellect and vision. His heart, which was a guarding tablet, meaning the source of preserving his knowledge, now itself becomes the Guarded Tablet (Al-Lawh Al-Mahfooz).

Al-Quran (85:22) Upon an imperishable tablet [inscribed] (Al-Lawh Al-Mahfooz).

Al-Lawh is something that is written on. Al-Lawh Al-Mahfooz, as in the aayah, (the Preserved Tablet) means, the place in the Heavens where the decrees of Allah﷾ are kept.

His soul becomes the guiding light, rather than his intellect as True Knowledge descends on his heart from Allah﷾.

Al-Quran (42:52) And thus, too, [O Muhammad,] have We revealed to you a life-giving message, [coming] at Our behest. [Before this message came unto you,] you did not know what revelation is, nor what faith [implies]: but [now] We have caused this [message] to be a light, whereby We guide whom We will of Our servants: and, verily, [on the strength thereof] you, too, shall guide [men] onto the straight way.

Intellect guided man on the path of this discovery but now, intellect itself becomes the pupil. Rumi gives the example of Angel Gibrail who was Prophet Muhammad'sﷺ first teacher.

However, he became powerless at one point in the face of Muhammad's﷽ ascent to the heavens, where he stopped. This was the furthest point in the Heavens, where no one was allowed to go except Prophet Muhammad﷽. Angel Gibrail stopped here saying he could not go further as his wings will catch fire, so the student surpassed the teacher in his spiritual and intellectual strength.

****

When the pen is of wind and the scroll of water,
Whatever you write perishes speedily.
It is written on water: if you seek constancy from it,
You will return biting your hands.
The wind in men is vanity and desire;
When you have abandoned vanity, is the message from Him.
Sweet are the messages of the Maker,
For it from head to foot is enduring.
The title for kings change, and their empire;
Except the empire and titles (insignia) of the prophets,
Because the pomp of kings is from vanity,
The glorious privilege of the prophets is from Majesty.
The names of kings are removed from the gold coins,
The name of Ahmad﷽ is stamped on them forever.
The name of Ahmad﷽ is the name of all the prophets;
When the hundred comes, ninety is with it as well.

All talk and writing that springs forth from the egoistic self is empty and transient, just like a pen of worldly desires writing on water. There is no reality or permanence to it. If the heart is emptied of selfish desires, the True Knowledge from the Almightyﷻ will descend and fill the heart with light. This message will have permanence and reliability.

Rumi goes on to say that the titles of kings and monarchs are also temporary because their power is from selfish desires and worldly goals, whereas the Prophets came from a Divine Ordinance. Their mission was for the greater good and higher truth. When a king dies his name is removed from the coins and other legislations, his followers are now behind a new ruler, but Prophets' legacies will remain till the end of time. Their death does not invalidate their jurisprudence. Even though the coming of one Prophet does invalidate the law of the previous Prophet, but it does not nullify his status. In fact, it is a continuum of the laws of the Almightyﷻ, and the name of all the prophets and Ahmed (Prophet Muhammadﷺ) will remain till eternity.

Rumi explains further that this specification of the name of Ahmed does not negate the previous Prophets as principally Prophet Muhammadﷺ is the epitome of perfection of all Prophets. The permanence of his religious law means the permanence of all previous religious laws. Rumi explains metaphorically that a 100 encompasses all numbers before it, so, if for example, you have 100 then you have 90 as well. In the same way, the name of Prophet Muhammadﷺ embodies all the Prophets before him.

****

The hare made much delay in going;

He rehearsed to himself the tricks.

The lion, incensed and wrathful and frantic,

Saw the hare coming from afar.

"Mercy!" cried the hare.

"I have an excuse, if your Lordship's pardon comes to my aid.

At breakfast-time I set out on the way,

I came towards the king with my comrade.

On the road a lion attacked your humble slave,

Attacked both us companions in travel who were coming.

I said to him, we are the slaves of the King of kings,

The lowly fellow-servants of that court.

He said, 'The King of kings! Who is he? Be ashamed!

Do not make mention of every base loon in my presence.

Both you and your king I will tear to pieces,

If you and your friend turn back from my door.'

We entreated him much: it was no use.

He seized my friend and left me to go alone."

"Come on in God's name," said the lion, "Let me see where he

is!

Go in front, if you are speaking truth,

That I may give him and a hundred like him

the punishment they deserve.

Or if this is a lie, that I may give your desserts to you."

The hare set out on the way, in front like a guide,

That he might lead him towards his snare,

Towards the well which he had designated;

He had made the deep well a snare for the lion's life.

The water bears a blade of straw to the plain;

How, I wonder, will the straw bear away a mountain?

The snare of his guile was a noose for the lion;

A marvellous hare, who was carrying off a lion!

A Moses draws Pharaoh, with his army and mighty host,

Into the river Nile;

A single gnat with half a wing

Cleaves intrepidly the suture of Nimrod's skull.

Rumi comes back to the story of the lion and the hare and how he tells a tale to ensnare the lion. The lion falls for his cunning plot and both head off for the well, which was to be the lion's trap. Look at the tiny hare and the enormous lion! Rumi says it is natural that water carries off blades of grass and straw with it, but here it seems a minor straw (hare) is carrying off a mountain (lion)!

Rumi shares two examples to give further strength to the surprising phenomenon of how size is irrelevant in the greater scheme of things. Prophet Moosa, with very little worldly prowess, lead the mighty pharaoh and his army into the Nile, where they all drowned. Nimrod was another powerful and evil king of ancient times who died because of a small gnat with only one wing that penetrated his skull.

****

Since the case is thus, begin humble supplication;
Set about lamenting and glorifying and fasting.
Lament continually, crying, "O You who well
know the hidden things,
Do not crush us beneath the stone of evil contrivance.
O Creator of the lion, if we have wrought evil and sinned,
Do not set the lion on us from the concealed place.
Do not give to sweet water the form of fire;
Do not put upon fire the form of water.
When You make drunk with the wine of Your wrath,
You give to things non-existent the form of existence."
What is drunkenness? That which binds the eye from eyesight,
So that a stone appears a jewel, and wool (pashm)
a jasper (yashm).
What is drunkenness? The perversion of the senses,
That change tamarisk-wood into sandal-wood in the sight.

Rumi says that since, with all our planning and strength, we cannot save ourselves from the vile enemy and predestination, turn to Allah﷾ and put your trust in Him. Use your knowledge and strategy but also plead to the Almighty﷾, glorify Him and ask for His help through supererogatory worship like fasting and supplication.

"O Allahﷻ! We have sinned and transgressed, but forgive us. Do not set the lion of ego and Satan upon us who are forever in ambush. They will trap us in our negligence and destroy us in this world and the Other World."

"O Lord of the Worldsﷻ! Do not take revenge for our transgressions as your pardon is filled with generosity. Do not make that which is beneficial to us, like sweet water, seem to our senses like fire, so that we run away from obedience and good deeds. And do not make sins and evil deeds, like fire, seem to us like cool water, sweet and attractive. This will result in making us see good deeds as dangerous and wickedness as beneficial. Please grant us insight so we can differentiate right from wrong and evil from good."

"O Allahﷻ! When your wrath annihilates the intellect, just as wine makes it transient and unstable, then things which have no good in them are perceived as beneficial and vice versa. The demise of intellect is a sign of the wrath of the Almightyﷻ.

Eyesight loses its insight so that a stone (useless pursuits) seems like a jewel (a thing of glory), and tamarisk wood (used for burning and carpentry) seems to appear like sandal (a kind of wood; its oil produces a distinctive fragrance that has been highly valued for centuries).

****

As soon as the lion and hare looked at the water in the well,

There shone forth in the water the light from the lion and him.

When the lion beheld his adversary in the water,

He left him and sprang into the well.

He fell into the well which he had dug,

Because his atrocity was coming on his own head.

The wickedness of evil-doers became a dark well;

So have said all the wise.

The more wicked one is, the more frightful is his well;

Justice has ordained worse for worse.

O you who from tyranny are digging a well,

You are making a snare for yourself.

Do not weave round yourself, like the silkworm.

You are digging a well for yourself: dig with moderation.

Deem not the weak to be without a champion;

recite from the Qur'an, When the help of God shall come.

Hence the lion met his just fate. The evil that he planned and executed on the jungle animals came back to him. To personify the well as the evil the lion plotted and the lion's actions as atrocity are metaphorical, as animals are not accountable for their actions.

Rumi transitions to sermonizing and says that the justice of the Almightyﷻ prescribes the worst punishment for the worst action.

As you plan evil and atrocities on the weak, so you are digging a deeper and deeper well of torture for yourself. Make sure you dig as much as you are capable of bearing, as none has the capacity to bear the wrath of Almighty. Cease in your evil ways.

You are like the silk worm, wrapping yourself in your silk, that is, your power and glory, till it will smother you to death.

Do not think the weak are without assistance. Rumi quotes the Quran when Allah helped Prophet Muhammad and the Muslims gain victory over the Quraysh, the strong and undefeatable people of Makka.

Al-Quran (110:1) When Allah's help comes, and victory.

THE ESSENCE OF ALL THESE VERSES IS REPROACHMENT OF OPPRESSION AND INJUSTICE.

****

The lion saw himself in the well, and in his fury
He did not know himself at that moment from the enemy.
Oh, many an evil that you see in others
Is your own nature in them, O reader!
In them shone forth all that you are
In your hypocrisy and injustice and insolence.
You are that, and you are striking those blows at yourself;
It is yourself you are cursing at that moment.
You are assaulting yourself, O simpleton,
Like the lion who made a rush at himself.
When you reach the bottom of your own nature,
Then you will know that that vileness was from yourself.
At the bottom it became manifest to the lion

That he who seemed to him to be another was his own image.

The Faithful are mirrors to one another;

This saying is related from the Prophet ﷺ.

If the true believer was not seeing by the Light of God,

How did things unseen appear naked to the true believer?

Inasmuch as you were seeing by the Fire of God,

You did not discern the difference between good and evil.

Little by little throw water on the fire,

That your fire may become light, O man of sorrow!

Throw, O Lord, the purifying water,

That this world-fire may become wholly light.

All the water of the sea is under Your command;

Water and fire, O Lord, are Yours.

If You will, fire becomes sweet water;

And if You will not, even water becomes fire.

This search in us is also brought into existence by You;

Deliverance from evil is Your gift, O Lord.

Without seeking You have given us this search,

You have given gifts without number and end.

Here Rumi transitions from the condition of the lion to the condition of the general humanity. Often people perceive malicious ethics or poor moral values in others, which are in reality within themselves. This can be in two ways.

One is when a person considers some failing in another which is actually his own defect. For example, a miserly person looks at a generous man, who for some reason refrained from spending at some point, and on the principle of "One measures according to his own measure", considers this as stinginess.

Second is when a sincere counsellor points out some flaw in Zayd, but Zayd perceives this as contempt and perverseness on the part of the counsellor because these are the qualities found within himself. Or, a just king ordains some deserved punishment to establish law and order but another perceives this as injustice and oppression due to his own ignorance and mindlessness.

Rumi exhorts to look within and know your own faults before pointing at others' faults, because when you point one finger at another, three of your own fingers are pointing at yourself.

Rumi dispels one misconception that might arise when sincere counsel is given by a mentor or guide. They also inform about the flaws in words and actions of the general public, so this would mean that the fault is within them too. Rumi says the difference here is that your perception is based on ego and self which can be at fault, whereas the accomplished and sincere guide's perception is based on selflessness and authenticity. There is little chance of a mistake. There is no personal motive, prejudice, ignorance or rage, but rather benevolence and sincerity for the protégé.

The Prophet said: The believer is a mirror to his faithful brother. He protects him against loss and defends him behind his back.

Abu Huraira said: "The believer is a mirror to his brother. If he sees something wrong in him, he should correct it."

The Messenger of Allah said: Beware of the intuition of the believer. Verily, he sees with the light of Allah. Then the

Prophetﷺ recited the verse, "Verily, in that are signs for those of discernment." (15:75)

Just as the seeker of the True Source sees with the light of Allahﷻ, your perception is from the light of the fire of egotism and selfish desires. To make your perception pure and clear, you need to extinguish this fire with the water of purity by searching your soul for the True Light, assuming the companionship of sincere and accomplished mentors and scholars. Then your despicable attributes will turn to praiseworthy qualities.

The previous verses explain how to extinguish the fire of selfish desires and the ego, which is a complex and difficult endeavor. Hence, Rumi pleads to the Almightyﷻ for help. This is also an allusion to the seeker that he should not rely only on his own knowledge and effort, nor be arrogant but always entreat Allahﷻ for guidance and mercy.

"O Lord, this desire to search for truth and light is also from you. This yearning is your bounty that has been bestowed on us without our seeking. Your mercy and blessings exceed beyond measure. Life, health, wealth, guidance, everlasting existence of the soul and innumerable hidden and manifest endowments are all from your grace. We can never count them as You have mentioned in the Quran."

Al-Quran (16:18) And if you would count Allah'sﷻ favors, you will not be able to number them; most surely Allahﷻ is Forgiving, Merciful.

If You grant so much without asking, then surely it is beyond doubt that You would not deny the one who pleads and supplicates.

Al-Quran (27:40) Everything is from the grace of our Lord.

This was exclaimed by Prophet Solomon☐ who realized that each blessing is a bounty of Allah, and that we will be tested by our blessings to see who are grateful and who are not.

****

"We have returned from the lesser jihad (warfare)
to the greater jihad."
This carnal self is Hell, and Hell is a dragon
Which is not diminished by oceans.
It would drink up the Seven Seas, and still
The blazing of that consumer of all creatures
would not become less.
Allah﷽ says, "Are you filled, are you filled?" It says, "Not yet;
Lo, here is the fire, here is the glow, here is the burning!"
It made a mouthful of and swallowed a whole world,
Its belly crying aloud, "Is there any more?"
Allah﷽, from where place is not, sets His foot on it;
Then it subsides at Be, and it was.
Only the straight arrow is put on the bow,
This bow has arrows bent back and crooked.
Be straight, like an arrow, and escape from the bow,

For without doubt every straight arrow will fly from the bow.

When I turned back from the outer warfare,

I set my face towards the inner warfare.

We have returned from the lesser Jihad,

We are engaged along with the Prophet in the greater Jihad.

I pray Allah to grant me strength and aid and pride,

That I may root up with a needle this mountain of Qaf.

As this story is about destroying an external foe, the lion, so Rumi transitions to the annihilation of the hidden foe, the carnal self. Striving against the ego and selfish desires is much bigger than fighting an apparent enemy because one is hidden and within while the other is discernable and outside oneself.

The literal meaning of Jihad is struggle or effort, and it means much more than holy war.

Muslims use the word Jihad to describe three different kinds of struggle:

- A believer's internal struggle to live out the Muslim faith as well as possible.

  Allah's Messenger said: "The strong is not the one who overcomes the people by his strength, but the strong is the one who controls himself while in anger."

- The struggle to build a good Muslim society.

  The Prophet said: "The one who strives to look after a widow or a poor person is like a warrior who fights for

Allah's⬥ Cause, or like him who performs prayers all the night and fasts all the day."

- Holy war: the struggle to defend Islam, with force if necessary.

The Messenger of Allah⬥ said: Verily! Setting out in the early morning or in the evening in order to fight in Allah's⬥ way is better than the world and what it contains.

Many modern writers claim that the main meaning of Jihad is the internal spiritual struggle, and this is accepted by many Muslims. However there are so many references to Jihad as a military struggle in Islamic writings that it is incorrect to claim that the interpretation of Jihad as holy war is wrong.

Rumi says it was easier for the hare to trick the lion and destroy him than for us to control our ego and carnal self. It is like Hell, never content; and Hell is personified as a dragon that can drink the water of all the oceans of the world and yet remain thirsty. The desires of the carnal self are never satiated as much as it gets from this world. The hare was like our reasoning intellect which is powerful in worldly affairs but has no power over the egoistic self. For one thing, it often has a hard time differentiating between virtue and vice; then it only has the power of analysis and thought but no strength of action.

Al-Quran (50:30) On that Day We will ask Hell, Are you filled? and it will answer, [Nay,] is there yet more [for me]?

The Prophet ﷺ said: The people will be thrown into the (Hell) Fire and it will say: 'Are there any more (to come)?' (50:30) till Allah ﷻ puts His Foot over it and it will say, 'Enough Enough!'

Just as Hell can only be controlled by the Almighty ﷻ, so He purges our carnal self and gives it peace from its unending desires of the ego. Who else can pull the bow of the ego than the Almighty ﷻ? Rumi uses the simile of bow for the egoistic self. There are three main characteristics of a bow.

One, it is difficult to pull and is used with great effort. Same is the ego which can only be controlled by the might of Allah ﷻ.

Two, straight arrows are shot from it which fly at great speed. Rumi says the egoistic self is the bow that shoots the arrows but they are not straight. Their path is unstable and erratic, depending only on selfish desires and motives.

Three, the arrows that are used in a bow have to be straight. Rumi says become a straight arrow guided by Divine Light so that you can fly from this bow of the ego on a straight path, rid yourself of its trickery and vice, and find peace and contentment.

Rumi says that after defeating the external foes, we are now focused on purification of the self and brightening the inner light of spirituality.

"I supplicate to Allah ﷻ for such metaphysical strength as is required for this humungous task so that I can overtake and control the ego. With Allah's ﷻ help and guidance and by following the Sunnah of the Holy Prophetﷺ I can dig up this Qaf (a mountain said to be near Iraq and associated with Middle Eastern mythology) with a needle; meaning I can defeat my ego in spite of my weaknesses and shortcomings."

Aameen

Thus ends Part 1 Book One of the Mathnavi

These are just five stories out of the total of 16 stories in Book One. I pray for guidance and strength to bring forth, in small doses, the rest of the stories from Book One. They are equally, if not more spiritually uplifting and intellectually stimulating. The commentary based on Kaleedi Mathnavi helped give clarity and depth to this glorious text.

The rest of the stories of Book One:

Story 6: Omar and the Ambassador

Story 7: The Merchant and his Clever Parrot

Story 8: The Harper

Story 9: The Arab and his Wife

Story 10: The Man who was Tattooed

Story 11: The Lion who Hunted with the Wolf and the Fox

Story 12: Joseph and the Mirror

Story 13: The Prophet's Scribe

Story 14: The Chinese and the Greek Artists

Story 15: Counsels of Reserve given by the Prophet to his Freedman Zaid

Story 16: Ali's Forbearance

Epilogue to Book One

This book is dedicated to:

My mother, who believed in me. She was the most gifted and authentic person I have known in my life.

My teacher and mentor Mufti Maulana Shafiq Arif and all my other honourable teachers who have shown me the True Path to a life well-lived.

My husband Taufiq, who showed me how to live life with patience and steadfastness.

My children, Kashif, Sana, Mairaj, Samira, Munir and Sahr who have helped me grow along with them.

My grandchildren, Muhammad, Aaizah, Sulaiman, Aaisha and Sitara, who filled my world with laughter and love. They energized me with all their joy and zest for life.

Every one of my beloved students whose passion to learn inspired me to teach.

My extended family and sincere friends whose love and support gave me strength.

This book would not have been possible without Team Al-Aaizah whose effort, contribution and support have been invaluable.

End Notes

[i] *Excerpt: The Masnavi I Manavi of Rumi Complete 6 Books Kindle Edition by Maulana Jalalu-'d-din Muhammad Rumi (Author), E.H. Whinfield (Translator), Publisher Orange Sky Project.*

[ii] *Lewis 2000, pp. 407–408*

[iii] *Lewis 2000, p. 408*

[iv] *Ibrahim Gamard, Rumi and Self Discovery, Dar al Masnav*

[v] Omid Safi https://renovatio.zaytuna.edu/article/sheath-your-sword APR 28, 2017, Retrieved June 12, 2019

[vi] Rumi: 53 Secrets from the Tavern of Love, trans. by Amin Banani and Anthony A. Lee, p. 3

[vii] Ibrahim Gamard (2004), *Rumi and Islam*, p. 163, ISBN 978-1-59473-002-3

[viii] *Ibrahim Gamard (2004), Rumi and Islam, SkyLight Paths, p. 169, ISBN 978-1-59473-002-3*

[ix] https://en.wikipedia.org/wiki/Rumi#cite_ref-81 Retrieved June 12, 2019

[x] https://en.wikipedia.org/wiki/Ashraf_Ali_Thanwi, Retrieved June 12, 2019

[xi] https://en.wikipedia.org/wiki/Platonic_love, Retrieved June 13, 2019

[xii] King, D. Brett (2009). The Roman Period and the Middle Ages. In King, D. B., Viney, W., Woody, W. D. (Eds.) A History of Psychology: Ideas and Context (4th ed., pp. 70–71) Boston, Massachusetts: Pearson Education, Inc.

[xiii] *The Masnavi I Manavi of Rumi Complete 6 Books Kindle Edition by Maulana Jalalu-'d-din Muhammad Rumi (Author), E.H. Whinfield (Translator), Publisher Orange Sky Project.*

[xiv] *The Masnavi I Manavi of Rumi Complete 6 Books Kindle Edition by Maulana Jalalu-'d-din Muhammad Rumi (Author), E.H. Whinfield (Translator), Publisher Orange Sky Project.*

[xv] Zarrinkoob, Abdol-Hosein (1970). "Persian Sufism in Its Historical

Perspective". *Iranian Studies.* **3** (3/4):
198. doi:10.1080/00210867008701404. JSTOR 4310072 *Retrieved from https://en.wikipedia.org/wiki/Abdal* June 13, 2019
[xvi] *Chabbi, J "Abdal" Encyclopedia Iranica. Archived from the original on 29 April 2011. Retrieved from https://en.wikipedia.org/wiki/Abdal* June 13, 2019
[xvii] https://en.wikipedia.org/wiki/Zopyrus, last edited on 20 January 2019, Retrieved June 13, 2019.
[xviii] *The Masnavi I Manavi of Rumi Complete 6 Books Kindle Edition by Maulana Jalalu-'d-din Muhammad Rumi (Author), E.H. Whinfield (Translator), Publisher Orange Sky Project.*
[xix] As above
[xx] *"Destruction of 'Adites' city". Madain Project. Retrieved from https://en.wikipedia.org/wiki/Ad June 14, 2019*
[xxi] Kalila and Dimna is a book containing a collection of fables. It was translated into Arabic in the Abbasid age specifically in the second hijri century by Abdullah ibn al-Muqaffa using his own writing style. Wikipedia
Originally published: 756 AD
Original language: Sanskrit
[xxii] *The Masnavi I Manavi of Rumi Complete 6 Books Kindle Edition by Maulana Jalalu-'d-din Muhammad Rumi (Author), E.H. Whinfield (Translator), Publisher Orange Sky Project.*
[xxiii] https://en.wikipedia.org/wiki/Amr_ibn_Hisham, Retrieved June 14, 2019

www.ingramcontent.com/pod-product-compliance
Lightning Source LLC
Chambersburg PA
CBHW061439150726
47987CB00001B/268